# MIST ON THE
# RICE-FIELDS

# MIST ON THE RICE-FIELDS

## A Soldier's Story of the Burma Campaign and the Korean War

by

# JOHN SHIPSTER

*When the mist was on the rice-fields*
*an' the sun was droppin' low,*
*She'd git 'er little banjo an' she'd sing 'Kulla-lo-lo!'*

Rudyard Kipling, Mandalay

LEO COOPER

First Published in Great Britain in 2000 by
LEO COOPER
an imprint of
Pen & Sword Books
47 Church Street
Barnsley
South Yorkshire
S70 2AS

A CIP record for this book is
available from the British Library.

ISBN 0 85052 742 2

Typeset in 11/13pt Sabon by
Phoenix Typesetting, Ilkley, West Yorkshire

Printed in England by Redwood Books Ltd,
Trowbridge, Wilts

# CONTENTS

# ACKNOWLEDGEMENTS

I am deeply indebted to friends and family who have been kind enough to read the manuscript and to offer comments and advice. I also thank the Imperial War Museum for their help in providing photographs. Above all I thank my wife Corry, without whose help and encouragement this book would not have been written.

**John Shipster**
*Woodbridge, Suffolk, 1999*

# INTRODUCTION
### *by*
### *His Honour Judge Robin Rowland QC*

As a friend of the author for more than 50 years I feel honoured to have been asked to write an introduction to this book. We first met in January 1943 in the 7th Battalion of the 2nd Punjab Regiment, Indian Army, which was then billeted in the rather unprepossessing quarter of Madras City called Washermanpet. Thus began an association that was to endure throughout our service together in the Far East, and which has happily survived down to the present day.

But our real association, and deeper friendship, started when the 7th Battalion, as part of 89 Indian Infantry Brigade of the 7th Indian Division, moved to the Arakan on the borders of India and Burma in the autumn of 1943 to begin the long campaign to recover Burma. This gives me some justification for aspiring to introduce this book. The Arakan sector of operations experienced the full cycle of defeat, partial recovery, renewed disappointment, and finally decisive victory. When the battalion arrived on this front in September the author, by then a company commander at the age of 21, was immediately thrust into action against the enemy. In Arakan, as later at Kohima and Manipur State, it was war against nature: torrential rain, mist, bitterly cold early mornings, mud and blazing sun. It was also war against an implacable and ferocious enemy: 'the ant-like soldier,' as General Sir William Slim described him. He fought most bravely and was devoted to what he conceived to be his duty. But he was a brutalized soldier. It was a savage war waged in the jungle. In times of peace the Arakan had its own strange beauty. In war it was evil: a place of treachery and terror. If men were brave in action, few witnessed it; if they had quit it would often have been unobserved.

As Lieut. Colonel Frank Owen, writer and editor, has observed: 'All depended on the soldier and how he bore himself, and each fighter had to conquer his own heart.'

In such circumstances, within the space of a few months the author was transformed from a green young officer into a battle veteran. In November, just weeks after his arrival in Arakan, he was shot and wounded by a Japanese sniper; on returning from hospital he was again severely wounded during the major Japanese Ha-Go offensive in February 1944. It was in these operations that he was awarded an Immediate DSO for outstanding gallantry and leadership a few days after his 22nd birthday.

This is not the place for an appreciation of the author's outstanding capability as a company commander in the Burmese jungle, but perhaps I might be permitted to pay a tribute to his unwavering responsibility towards himself, his soldiers, and his regiment. Gifted as he was with great powers of leadership, he was also a keen observer of people, places and events around him. In this book he has written a personal and subjective account of how the war in Burma affected him, and the reader will find not only vivid descriptions of life and, indeed, death in the jungle but also broad splashes of humour born of a sense of wit that characterizes many of the stories he has to tell. It seems to me that it was this same lively sense of the ridiculous that served to sustain him and those he commanded in battle in Burma and later in life.

Another remarkable talent of my old friend has been his ability to look forward, to forgive his former enemies for the many atrocities committed by them under the cult of *Bushido*. He has embraced the spirit of reconciliation with enthusiasm in a way that is a lesson to us all. Neither the power to hate nor the lust to kill were ever naturally part of his armour in his battles against the Japanese. As he himself writes: 'Many of us who fought in Burma do not harp on yesterdays nor can we see any future in maintaining a non-forgiving attitude.'

With gratitude and affection, therefore, I wish this book success, and its author – with his wife Corry – every happiness for many years to come.

# FOREWORD
*by*
*Fergal Keane*

We live in an age where the virtues of courage and sacrifice are too often ignored in favour of the cynical and the vulgar. Our popular culture celebrates ostentatious wealth, it exalts the trivial. What a pleasure it is then to contemplate the life of a man who represents values we might easily imagine had vanished in the all-pervasive rush of the greedy society. John Shipster is one of a quiet breed of heroes. Let me quickly add that he would immediately throw his eyes up to heaven if I were to mention the word hero in front of him; for he is the most modest of men. It is a modesty familiar to any who have spent time in conversation with the veterans of Britain's two great wars of the 20th century.

Having spent some time in war zones I have some limited idea of the terror and pity of modern warfare. But, of course, nothing in my experience can match what young men from Britain experienced when they were despatched to Flanders in 1914 or to face the might of the Japanese Imperial Army in Burma in 1941. This was total warfare and, unlike the war correspondent, the soldier could not turn and walk away at the end of the day, he could not seek refuge far behind the front lines when the going got heavy. To those who have experienced war the early realization that your life may at any moment be extinguished can be petrifying. To live with that realization for hour after hour, day after day, week after week. . . . I find it hard to contemplate the reality of such a predicament.

When I asked John Shipster about this, he answered typically, 'Well, one just got on with things.' This is not proof of some inner coldness, nor does it suggest that the men who fought in Burma in those terrible battles around Kohima were conditioned to fight like automatons. Remember they were young men, many of them in battle for the first time. It is simply – as you will discover when you read this memoir – that survival depended on staying focused entirely on the task at hand. Over the years I have read many accounts of the fighting in Burma and am glad to say that John Shipster's memoir can take a proud place with the best. In the pages that follow, you will read a riveting and deeply moving account of warfare at its most brutal. The author does not shy away from the horror of close-quarter combat, but neither does he allow his prose to lapse into the indulgent or the speculative. What we get are the facts: harrowing and inspiring.

I met John Shipster through his son, my good friend Michael, a Foreign Office diplomat whom I first met in South Africa during the transition from apartheid to majority rule. Michael had told me that his father was writing an account of his service in the Burma Campaign and later in the Korean War. As a keen reader of books about the Second World War, I was delighted to read the manuscript. As a writer I was immediately impressed by John Shipster's ability to transform his experiences into clear and engaging prose. More impressive still was the restraint in the writing; in a narrative where there would have been justification for extravagant language John Shipster resists the temptation.

We are also given a wonderful sense of the landscape through which the young officer travelled, firstly in India, then through the Burma campaign and also in Korea where he witnessed the Chinese entry into the war. His love of the Indian sub-continent is evident throughout and the return to his regimental depot many long years after the war is beautifully described.

Born in 1922, John Shipster was educated at Marlborough College and at the age of eighteen he enlisted into the 2nd Punjab Regiment at Meerut. With Japanese armies sweeping through the Pacific and also advancing towards India from Burma, the young officer was sent with his infantry company to the Arakan in north-west Burma. I will leave the descriptions of the fighting to the author himself – no second-hand telling could possibly do justice to the intensity of the experience he describes. Twice wounded, he was awarded an 'Immediate' DSO before finding himself commanding his old company during the last three weeks of the siege of Kohima.

In February 1945 he was again wounded after landing by canoe on what he thought was an unoccupied island in the Irrawaddy River. But he returned to the battalion in time to take part in the final rout and ultimate surrender of the Japanese. His subsequent career would see him serve in Hong Kong, Korea, with Nato Forces in Fontainebleau in France, Germany, Northern Ireland, Guyana, on attachment to the US army in America during the Vietnam War, and in Belize. For his service in Belize he was made a CBE.

After such a life – crowded with incident and adventure – one might forgive John Shipster if he were to indulge in a little self-importance, but there is not a trace of vanity or pomposity about the man. He is modest to a fault with a well-developed sense of fun. The hours that I have spent in his company I will treasure: he has shown me the value of courage and consistency. This book is a testament to the valour of many men; it also reminds us of a sacrifice that succeeding generations must never forget.

PROLOGUE

## Reconciliation

In November 1990 I was fortunate to be included in a small group of Burma veterans who visited Japan at the invitation of our Japanese counterparts. It was only the second such visit since the end of World War II. The purpose was to create better understanding between ourselves and our formidable opponents, who fought against us over a half century ago in the longest campaign of the war, and one that was surely the hardest and cruellest. My own experience of some two years of fighting seems sometimes as close as yesterday, so it came somewhat of a shock that at that time, approaching nearly 70 years of age, I found myself the youngest member of our party. Not unnaturally our opponents had changed and aged too. In my mind I have had over the years an unvarying picture of dead Japanese soldiers wearing their distinctive helmets on shaven heads and dressed in blood-stained khaki uniforms, many carrying on their packs the vivid crimson national emblem of the Rising Sun.

Our visit had been made possible by the generosity of our hosts, who financed every aspect of our travels. Our party of twelve encompassed a 'broad church', coming from both the British and Indian Armies, and included two who had worked as POWs on the infamous Siam–Burma railway, associated in so many people's minds with the film *The Bridge over the River Kwai*. Others included a Major-General (author on the Burma War), a Canadian Spitfire pilot, Louis Allen, the distinguished Burma War historian, an ex-regular RSM from the Royal Welsh Fusiliers and a bagpipe-playing Brigadier from the Argyll and Sutherland Highlanders, who piped us around Japan, causing much amusement among our Japanese

1

hosts. The one thing that we all had in common was that we had spent our youth in combat in 'The Forgotten War'.

The Japanese are estimated to have had overall 400,000 casualties in Burma, of whom 150,000 died. They often chose death by suicide using a hand grenade rather than face the ignominy of capture. The differences between the Burma campaign and modern high-tech warfare are stark indeed. Our mobility was our feet. Combat was generally a personal affair, and guided weapons belonged only to science fiction; even helicopters were unknown. Malaria was a scourge.

I have lived for some years in East Anglia, where there is still a very strong anti-Japanese feeling. This is understandable; the 18th East Anglian Division landed in Singapore just prior to its capture in November 1941 and were immediately 'put in the bag' without having the opportunity to acquit themselves in battle. The majority were eventually put to work on the Siam–Burma railway, where they suffered terrible hardships and many died, but I am sure that their hatred is in part accentuated by the ignominy of their capture. Sadly it will only go when they die, unless they can find it in their hearts to forgive.

After a 14-hour flight we landed at Narita Airport, some 30 miles from Tokyo. In the early morning sunshine we had a wonderful view of the sacred snow-capped Mount Fuji. A group of Japanese veterans met us carrying Union Jacks, which in some cases were larger than themselves. (We were struck by the fact that younger generations of Japanese today are some 3 to 4 inches taller than those we fought against. This, I am told, is because they now eat more protein.)

Our ten-day trip was confined to Honshu Island, the largest. We were based in Tokyo, but visited Hiroshima, Okayama, Kyoto and Yokohama. We also visited the beautiful Commonwealth War Graves cemetery near Yokohama, where there are about seventy-five graves of soldiers from my former British regiment, The Middlesex, who died as POWs, after having been taken prisoner after the fall of Hong Kong in December 1941.

During our visit we travelled many miles, met many veterans and attended numerous functions. We were also invited into their homes to meet their families and have a meal. One particularly memorable event was our invitation to lunch in a large hall near the Imperial

Palace in Tokyo. After lunch we were ushered onto the stage of a large theatre and confronted by approximately 1,200 veterans. The Japanese veterans stood up and, to our amazement and embarrassment, applauded for nearly three minutes. Later, after speeches, we exited down a central aisle while a Japanese version of 'Auld Lang Syne' was played. We were all very much taken aback by the emotions shown by these hardened old soldiers, for many had tears streaming down their faces, and we were not too steady either. But then our Brigadier bagpiper cranked up his pipes and tears soon changed to laughter.

Later, in the foyer of the theatre, we were introduced to a charming old lady, the widow of General Kimura, the Japanese Commander-in-Chief in Burma, who had been executed for war crimes. She said that she wished to meet in friendship the former enemies of her husband. What courage on her part.

When we flew back from Narita Airport one of Japan's most famous Burmese veterans (Major Nishida), who had fought at Kohima and was at that time within 300 yards of my Company's position, came to see me off. He gave me a lavish present for my wife, a silver brooch with cultured pearls. Previously, when nude bathing in hot sulphur springs, he had shown me where six Sten gun bullets had entered his body. He jokingly remarked that perhaps my soldiers had shot him.

My visit to Japan ended a cycle in my life. Many of us who fought in Burma do not harp on yesterdays, although I appreciate that some people do look backwards and are unable to forgive or forget. They have their own reasons and they are entitled to their views. Those of us who went to Japan in a spirit of 'burying the hatchet' do not share those views, nor can we see any future in maintaining a non-forgiving attitude.

Probably the best-known exponent of Japanese reconciliation is the writer and philosopher Laurens van der Post, who was taken prisoner by the Japanese in the Far East in 1942 and remained in a prisoner-of-war camp in Java (Indonesia) until the Japanese surrender in August 1945. In his compelling book *The Seed and the Sower*,* later made into a successful film *Merry Christmas, Mr*

---

* Laurens Van der Post, *The Seed and the Sower* (Hogarth, 1963).

*Lawrence*, he described his experiences, particularly those affecting the souls of men. His was a battle for survival amidst contrasting wills and philosophies. On one occasion van der Post was sentenced to death and led out to be executed by beheading with a military sword, but at the very last moment was reprieved. Yet out of all the violence and misery, strong bonds of friendship were formed between captors and captives.

A more recent writer has been Eric Lomax, who wrote *The Railway Man*,* an extraordinary story of torture and reconciliation, which around the time of the 50th anniversary of the victory over Japan (VJ Day) was made into a most moving TV film. John McCarthy, himself held hostage in the Lebanon for some years, wrote: 'I turned the last page weeping tears of sorrow, pride and gratitude.'


## The Japanese Soldier

Looking back over 50 years, I cannot remember ever having been told anything about the Japanese during our training in India before we went to Burma. I was ignorant of the Japanese soldier's traditional background and culture, ignorant too of his psyche and the ethos that governed both his personal and military behaviour. I knew nothing of the cult of Emperor worship, nor of the soldier's willingness to die rather than be taken prisoner, which accounted in part for the scorn and derision with which the Japanese treated all prisoners.

As the months passed I did of course learn the significance of words such as *banzai* (Japanese battle cry and salute to 'The Emperor') and *hara-kiri* (ceremonial suicide by ripping open the belly, substituted in battle by clasping a hand grenade to the stomach). I am certain that our soldiers, both British and Indian, were handicapped by their lack of knowledge about the Japanese soldier, and initially regarded him as some sort of super 'bogey-man'. British soldiers who disembarked from troopships at Singapore in late 1941 and almost immediately became prisoners of

* Eric Lomax, *The Railway Man* (London: Jonathan Cape, 1995).

war had had no indoctrination whatsoever. They were even ignorant that rice was the staple diet in the Far East, and through a mixture of ignorance and prejudice sometimes refused to eat rice even though it was essential for their own survival.

In September 1948, in the aftermath of the war, a meeting was held at Chatham House, London, with the aim of trying to define the 'Japanese military character'. Those present included General Slim (Commander 14th Army) and General Percival (Commander in Singapore at the time of its surrender). A number of experienced Japanese-speaking British diplomats were also present. Both generals acknowledged the individual courage of Japan's servicemen and attributed it to their patriotism and devotion to the Emperor. When called upon to do so, the Japanese really did fight to 'the last man and the last round'. General Slim cited Japanese suicide attacks on tanks* and the killing of their own wounded soldiers rather than letting them become prisoners. The question of atrocities in China was raised and it was the opinion that when these did occur they were the result of a general policy rather than a breakdown in unit discipline.

Throughout the Burma campaign 150,000 Japanese were killed, but we took only 1,700 prisoners, including many who were sick, and the majority of these were captured in the last few months of the war. No officer was captured above the rank of major.**

In 1950 I was serving in Hong Kong with the 1st Battalion The Middlesex Regiment (The Diehards) when we were sent to Korea to join United Nations forces in the war against the North Koreans and later the Chinese. The Diehards had fought most gallantly against the Japanese in Hong Kong in 1941. All those not killed were taken prisoner. There were in the Battalion a number of soldiers who had been prisoners throughout the war, and all were badly treated, but stressed that the most cruel guards were often the Koreans and not the Japanese. Cruelty was, however, accentuated by low-grade Japanese officers and NCOs having a pretty free rein as to how to

* Japanese soldiers would lie in slit trenches in the path of advancing tanks, exploding their mines when the tanks were directly above them and killing themselves in the process.
** Louis Allen, *Burma: The Longest War 1941–45* (Dent, 1984).

maintain discipline. Punishments in the POW camps were severe. When 'in the field' punishments in the Japanese Army were also severe. Cowardice was punishable by death; lesser crimes were usually punished by making the culprit stand to attention all night holding his weapon, and minor offences by striking a soldier across the face.

On leaving Korea in 1951 I returned to Hong Kong via Japan where, on an American air base, I met a former Japanese colonel who spoke good English. I asked him how it was that the Japanese Army committed so many atrocities during what has become known as the Rape of Nanking in 1937, when many thousands of innocent civilians were executed, raped and burnt. His answer was interesting. He said that in private the Japanese soldier lived a life of complete regulation, complying with rituals both at home and outside the home, and of course with the rituals of his Buddhist or Shinto faith. When free of these fetters the soldiers simply 'cut loose'. I have doubts about this explanation and think that it was an act to deliberately terrorize the Chinese. I am inclined, therefore, to side with the opinions of General Slim and General Percival.

Japanese cruelty is well documented, not only as regards the last war but also in their subjugation of the Koreans and Chinese. It is a strange paradox that there is also in the Japanese military character a strong sense of chivalry, which was displayed by their troops in China during the Boxer Rebellion (1899–1901) and in particular by their treatment of Russian POWs during the Russian–Japanese War at the turn of the century. It is interesting that the Japanese Navy, with its strong Royal Navy connections, has always had a strong code of honour.

Finally I should mention two points that were recently expressed by a Mr Hirakubo, now a resident in this country, but formerly an officer in the Japanese Army, who fought at Kohima. I know Mr Hirakubo personally as a man of the highest integrity, who in 1994 was awarded an OBE by Her Majesty the Queen in recognition of his efforts to promote Anglo-Japanese reconciliation. In one of his talks in London to Burma veterans he said that:

Japanese families considered themselves to be branches of their Royal Family to whom they believed they were related. The

Emperor was considered to be divine. All this came to an abrupt end when Japan surrendered and the Emperor renounced his divinity. It is almost impossible for a non-Japanese to appreciate the enormous shock this was to the population as a whole.

*Chapter 1*

# A PRELUDE TO WAR

## Introduction

My father, having got an engineering degree at the University of London, went out to Burma in 1907 to work with a general trading company. He returned to England before World War I, joined the Army, served in France, was badly wounded, and awarded a Military Cross. He later became a regular officer in the Royal Tank Regiment and died of cancer in September 1941 while still serving.

My father was educated at Marlborough College, as were two of his three brothers, during the latter part of Queen Victoria's reign. One brother, Walter, became a regular Army officer, won a Military Cross in France and was killed by a Turkish sniper on the road from Jerusalem to Nazareth just a few weeks before the end of World War I. Of the two remaining brothers, one was commissioned into the Royal Navy and the other went to Australia to establish a vineyard. At the outbreak of World War I he joined the Australian Expeditionary Force.

I was born in January 1922 at St Leonards-on-Sea, Sussex. My schooling was relatively undistinguished, but I was happy both at preparatory school and at Marlborough. I played all games with moderate success and managed to pass the Oxford and Cambridge matriculation exam. I found no difficulty in readily accepting the discipline of school and the hierarchical system of management. I suppose I must have been a round peg in a round hole and I am firmly convinced that my liberal but disciplined schooling made my sudden transition from school to the Indian Army relatively easy.

In 1939 life at Marlborough went on as much as usual, but the omens of possible war with Germany were on the horizon. In March

German forces entered Czechoslovakia and six months later, on 1 September, Germany invaded Poland. At that time I was on a family holiday in Southern Ireland and my father decided to return to England immediately. I clearly remember listening with my mother to Prime Minister Neville Chamberlain's declaration of war on Germany on 3 September 1939 and feeling excited. I was then aged 17½. At that time I thought that I would join the Army and hope to get a commission. To me it seemed obligatory to join up as soon as possible after leaving Marlborough at the end of the summer term 1940.

In various ways our lives at school changed. We were issued with gas masks and warned of the possibility of gas attacks from the air. The City of London School was evacuated to Marlborough and the pupils were billeted in the town, but they shared our classrooms on a rota system. Petrol was rationed and in consequence my parents were no longer able to visit me, but perhaps the worst inconvenience was the 100 per cent blackout at night.

After the outbreak of war, Sandhurst, the officer cadet training academy, ceased commissioning regular officers and my father wrote to tell me that there was a scheme whereby public schoolboys with good records and strongly recommended by their headmasters could be enlisted and go out to India to be commissioned in the rapidly expanding Indian Army. I discussed this with my father and decided to apply. I reported with some trepidation to the nearest recruiting office, passed my medical examination and was enlisted into the Royal Scots, along with many others who were going out to India as potential officer cadets. The reason for enlisting in the Royal Scots was that we had to be badged to an infantry regiment and the Royal Scots were sending out a large draft to India.

My parents' calm influence led me to accept events as a natural course. Certainly I was excited and looked on the future with a sense of adventure. At this time the war had not reached India and the future was unknown. I was ready to face it wherever it might lead. Little did I know that the war was to last five years and engulf half the world. Nor could I foresee that I would never see my father again. So began my 'rites of passage' from schoolboy to veteran.

## Enlistment in the Army and Voyage to India

I left Marlborough in the summer of 1940, soon after the fall of France. My excitement was tinged with sadness at leaving the school where I had been so happy. August and September saw the massed air raids on Britain, now known as the Battle of Britain, in which the Germans lost their air superiority. I remember seeing some of the air battles, with the smoke trails weaving across the clear summer skies and the tremendous thrill on hearing that on one particular day our Hurricane and Spitfire fighters had shot down 140 German planes. I knew at this time that, provided I passed the necessary interview and medical examination, I would be going to India to be commissioned into the rapidly expanding Indian Army. I had always wanted to go into the Army and this scheme offered an early opportunity to get a commission. The one problem was that, although India had entered the war, there was no military activity along her frontiers and it might look as if I was 'escaping' by going there. No one could then foresee the disasters that lay ahead, with Japan's entry into the war leading to the fall of Singapore and Hong Kong and the capture of Burma.

I spent July and August working first on a farm in Wiltshire and then on a Forestry Commission project on Exmoor (I cycled from North London to Exmoor). The one excitement was seeing a German Heinkel bomber crash into a wood and then being apprehended by a local policeman who thought I was a German crew member trying to escape on a bicycle. In September I passed my medical and interview for the Indian Army and was enlisted as a private soldier in the Royal Scots. It was not until mid-November that the long-awaited instructions finally arrived and I was told to report to Willems Cavalry Barracks at Aldershot. I said goodbye to my mother and did not see her again for 5½ years. My father drove me to Aldershot; I remember that our farewell was short, for we were both nervous of sentimentality and knew that we might not meet again.

The time spent in this antiquated Victorian barracks was probably one of the most unpleasant periods of my life. The living conditions were appalling; there were twenty-four soldiers in one barrack room, heated by only one small coal fire in bitterly cold weather, with nowhere to sit and read or write. There were no indoor recreational facilities. I seemed to spend the whole time on cookhouse fatigues – cleaning vegetables, washing up in tepid, greasy water and help- ing to prepare uneatable food. To add to the misery, the NCOs appeared to enjoy making life as difficult as possible. The difficul- ties were compounded by the fact that, as we were strangers to each other and did not belong to a proper unit, we had not had time to establish that corporate comradeship and sense of humour that are so essential when things are bad. The one consolation was that I was proud of my Royal Scots badge and liked wearing my Balmoral Highland headdress.

In December we were placed under orders to 'stand by to move'. For security reasons our mail was censored and we were not allowed to leave the Aldershot area. We were forbidden to talk about the fact that we were destined to go to India. German submarines were already inflicting heavy losses on our shipping in the Atlantic and any advance information of impending convoy movements would be of inestimable value to them. The issue of pith helmets and tropical clothing was also, of course, secret. A dreary Christmas came and went. On Boxing Day orders were received that we were to move by train the following day. We entrained on 27 December, still not knowing where we were going. The train journey provided a splendid guessing game, for there were no place names on the rail- way stations through which we passed. Our money was on Liverpool.

In the event, after a 12-hour journey, we passed through Glasgow and arrived at Greenock on the Clyde, where we embarked that night on the Royal Mail ship *Highland Chieftain*, a former passenger-cum-cargo boat used exclusively for importing frozen meat from Rio de Janeiro and Montevideo on the River Plate. She was only 14,000 tons with a top speed of 15 knots. Normally she was able to accommodate about 180 first- and second-class passengers, but, having been converted for troop carrying, she now had about 1,200 all ranks aboard. Once aboard we seemed to be isolated from the whole world. There was no news and we had no outside contact. We remained in Greenock for a further two days, but on the third day silently slipped our moorings and sailed away. It was about one month before my 19th birthday and little did I realize that I would not see England again until I was 24. Next morning we awoke to find that we were about 120 miles out in the

Atlantic and forming up in a large convoy of approximately thirty ships with a big naval escort. We became part of what was termed a 'fast convoy' (14 knots), carrying troops and essential war equipment to India and the Far East.

Life aboard was far from easy. We slept in hammocks above our mess decks, with absolutely no privacy. The ablutions and latrines were of the most primitive sort. The galleys had been hastily improvised and it was obvious that the cooks had had no training. The daily routine began with stowing away our hammocks and preparing the mess decks for breakfast. After breakfast, whenever possible, we went in small groups for physical exercise on the boat deck. I had two additional duties. First, I became batman to an unpleasant young officer in the Royal Scots who was later killed in Singapore. Second, I took my turn at manning one of the Lewis anti-aircraft machine-guns; stupidly, someone thought that, as I had had some limited Army training in the officer training corps at school, I could fire a Lewis gun. Fortunately, we had no air attacks and when we were well out in the Atlantic the Lewis guns were stowed away and I took my turn as a submarine spotter on a platform up one of the masts, with a direct telephone to the bridge. During the whole voyage the only report that I made turned out to be whales, which at a distance looked remarkably like submarines. At night all ships were totally blacked out and we seemed to be sailing in splendid isolation. In warmer weather the blacked-out portholes made it stiflingly hot below deck.

Our first port of call was Freetown in Sierra Leone, a British colony since 1787 and once known as the 'white man's grave' because of the poor climate and a lethal cocktail of life-threatening fevers. Freetown had the best harbour in the whole West African coast and while there we took on fresh water and oil. It was pleasant to see land again and the local Africans surrounding the ship in their small dugout canoes trying to sell us fruit made a pretty picture.

After leaving Sierra Leone we went around the Cape of Good Hope to Durban, where we stopped for three days and were allowed ashore. It was a memorable visit because of the hospitality of the South Africans, who took us to their houses and made us very welcome. It was marvellous to be able to walk into a good hotel and have a first-class meal. South Africa gave every impression of being a land of plenty.

At Durban we said goodbye to the *Highland Chieftain* and boarded the *Athlone Castle* (Union Castle Line) for the remainder of our journey to Bombay. The explanation that we were given was that conditions on the *Highland Chieftain* had become intolerable. We were delighted, for our new home seemed like a luxury hotel compared with what we had been used to. At the same time we were sad to say goodbye to our old ship; within her dirty bulk we had developed a strong corporate spirit and, surprisingly, had found much to laugh about. From Durban we sailed for Bombay, but rumours of a German raider in the Indian Ocean forced us to change course to seek the safety of the anchorage at Mombasa.

After three days of sanctuary there we sailed for Bombay without our former convoy, arriving at the end of February after a total voyage of nearly eight weeks. The voyage was largely uneventful. One event of interest after leaving Zanzibar was that in the middle of the Indian Ocean we hit a whale, which was sporting itself across our bows, and I saw it washed astern in a sea of blood. Another strange event was that, when we were approaching Bombay, I saw a sea snake about 12 feet in length swimming on the surface of the sea. These large snakes are more common around the Indian coast than elsewhere. They have a considerable girth and are venomous.

There can be few more beautiful and impressive sights than the approach to Bombay from the sea, up the waterway studded with hilly islands, with the stately buildings of the city in the background. In the distance we could see the peaks of the Western Ghats.

## Bombay

In 1941 Bombay was the capital of a vast province called the Bombay Presidency, comprising both British India and fifty-one Indian states; also included in its jurisdiction was Aden. Today Bombay is the capital of Maharashtra and has expanded its population five times to 7 million, and in so doing has produced some of the world's worst slums. Bombay was India's major port and known as the Gateway to India. There is in fact a triumphal arch of that name, built to commemorate the visit to India in 1911 of King George V and Queen Mary, who were later crowned as Emperor and Empress of India.

After disembarking we had a whole day to spend in Bombay before making the train journey to Bangalore in Mysore State. The sudden impact of this vast city was confusing to say the least. The streets and pavements teemed with vehicles and masses of people; general hubbub and noise permeated everywhere. If I had not been in the company of my friends I would certainly have found it very alarming. After being aboard ship for so long, we were also assailed by a rich mixture of smells, ranging from spices to garbage. The locals' overt hawking, spitting and nose-blowing through the fingers added to our general amusement. We were constantly solicited by *tonga wallahs* (pony cart drivers), shopkeepers and guides. Our general appearance did not help; we looked quite appalling, as our standard issue private soldiers' uniform did not fit us and we had had no laundry services for two months other than what we handwashed ourselves. The Indian soldiers, by contrast, looked immaculately clean and all officials, whether European or Indian, looked as if they had come straight off a parade ground. I remember going into Bombay's premier hotel, the Taj Mahal, to order a beer and being regarded with complete disdain by the Europeans there.

## India in 1941

In 1941 India was the 'jewel in the crown' of the British Empire. It was a vast country of some 500 million people, part of the greatest empire that the world has ever seen, on which the sun, it was thought, would never set. Generations of soldiers, adventurers, businessmen and administrators had served and worked there to keep the *pax Britannica* in the Empire's proudest possession. Hindus and Muslims lived together, for Pakistan had not yet been born as a result of Independence. India was then composed of British India and 565 Indian States, large and small, ruled by maharajahs, rajahs and nawabs, who each had an average of 11 titles, 5.8 wives, 12.6 children, 9.2 elephants, 2.8 railway cars, 3.4 Rolls-Royces and 22.9 tigers killed!*

India was not at war in the real meaning of the word, although

---

* Larry Collins and Dominique Lapierre, *Freedom at Midnight* (London: Collins, 1975).

Indian units were serving with distinction in the Western Desert in North Africa. Pearl Harbor, and the consequent advance of the Japanese armies to the very borders of India, was yet to come. Life in India had hardly been affected by the war. Servants were plentiful and one could live like a king on a pittance. For those in the Army it was a sportsman's paradise. What struck me most forcibly was the great poverty of so many people and the continual seeking of alms by beggars, many of whom had appalling deformities, often self-inflicted in order to solicit sympathy.

## Bangalore Officer Cadet School

Our first night in Bombay was spent aboard ship. Early the following morning we departed on the 600-mile rail journey to Bangalore, the capital of Mysore in the centre of Southern India. We travelled in third-class carriages with plain, hard wooden seats. The journey took about 20 hours. There was nowhere to sleep and anyway we had no bedding. Nevertheless I enjoyed the journey, for I was fascinated by the countryside and the towns and villages through which we passed.

Bangalore was a pleasant city with a good climate, being situated some 3000 feet above sea level. In 1941 it had the largest military cantonment in Southern India. There were about 600 officer cadets who had travelled out from England, mostly straight from public schools. We were organized into platoons and companies. Our instructors were all British and came from both the British and Indian Armies. It was a sort of mini-Sandhurst and the penalty for failing the course was to be sent to a British battalion in the rank of private soldier.

Our living conditions were far better than anything we had pre-viously experienced. We lived in wooden huts divided up into two-bedded rooms; each cadet had a bed plus mosquito net, desk, chair, bookcase and chest of drawers. Between the huts were the ablution blocks with cold showers and bucket-type latrines; these were emptied by the sweepers, who patiently waited for the *sahibs* to deposit their excreta. I remember being asked after arrival if I was a *hazri ke pahle wallah* or a *hazri ke b'ad wallah*: that is, did I perform before or after breakfast? For every two rooms there was a 'room bearer' who looked after the rooms and polished our military kit. My room-companion was a most pleasant chap, David Piper, who in England had been training to be a ballet dancer; after the war he had a distinguished career and received a knighthood for his services to the arts. My bearer was a Tamil called Madri, who told me he was a Christian, which probably meant that he had previously been an 'untouchable' and had converted to Christianity in order to escape the Hindu caste system.

The cadets' mess seemed like paradise after the rigours of our voyage out to India: spacious and cool, with overhead fans. The food was good too, particularly the wide variety of fruit, some of which I had never seen before. Once a week we dined formally, drinking the loyal toast to 'The King Emperor'. Overall, life was pleasant, but socially there was little or no opportunity to make contact with the British population, military or civilian. I think we were looked upon as some sort of outcasts, who were on the same rung of the social ladder as British Other Ranks, with whom I had a great deal of sympathy for they had little or no social compatibility with the local communities. A few of us obtained horses on loan from the Mysore Lancers; I had a splendid horse by the name of Shamshudin, which I rode on every possible occasion in the surrounding countryside. It cost the equivalent of £1 a week for the loan; the cost of the feed was minimal and three of us shared a *sais* (groom).

Our training lacked any sort of realism and, although at the time we seemed to be working hard, with hindsight there was no real feeling of urgency in what we did. There was an acute shortage of transport and we went everywhere on issued bicycles. I never saw a military radio set at Bangalore; all our signals training was done using the Morse code, either with an Aldis signalling lamp or with semaphore flags, which I never used again after leaving Bangalore. Much of our tactical training was to do with the drills of picketing on the North-West Frontier. Modern mechanized warfare was mentioned only briefly and jungle warfare was not taught at all. The one subject that was taught thoroughly was 'Duties in aid of the Civil Power', that is, riot drills. There was an acute shortage of ammunition, both live and blank, so on exercises we simulated firing by whirling wooden rattles or waving small flags.

Midway through the course we had a week's break and I was fortunate enough to spend the time with the parents of one of my study companions at Marlborough, Brigadier and Mrs Westmacott (he was affectionately known in the Indian Army as Tum Tum Westmacott). Peter, their son, was with me at Bangalore. We went to Mysore, where we stayed in the guest house of the Maharajah, and were among his personal guests at one of the great Hindu religious festivals, Dashera: this was a festival lasting ten days in honour of Durga, the Goddess of War. While there we fished in the Nilgiri Hills, visited a tea plantation and saw wild young elephants being corralled in a giant *keddah* (a wooden stockade). One evening we motored through a part of the Mysore jungles and saw in our headlights *chital* (small deer) and *nilgai* (slate-blue large antelope). I returned to Bangalore refreshed and enthusing about the wonderful diversity of India.

Our thoughts now began to be directed towards our commissioning, which was to be on 10 September. I knew that I had a reasonable chance of going into a good infantry regiment, for my general gradings were above average, but sadly I had no contacts in the Indian Army to whom I could turn for advice.

The various regiments all had for me such emotive and romantic names. In order of seniority they were:

| | |
|---|---|
| 1st Punjab | 12th Frontier Force |
| 2nd Punjab | 13th Frontier Force Rifles |
| 4th Bombay Grenadiers | 14th Punjab |
| 5th Mahratta Light Infantry | 15th Punjab |
| 6th Rajputana Rifles | 16th Punjab |
| 7th Rajput | 17th Dogra |
| 8th Punjab | 18th Royal Garhwal Rifles |
| 9th Jat | 19th Hyderabad |
| 10th Baluch | 10 regiments of Gurkha Rifles |
| 11th Sikh | |

In the event I was commissioned into the 7/2nd Punjab Regiment (that is, the seventh Battalion of the second Punjab Regiment), stationed in Meerut, not far from Delhi.

My commissioning day, which I was so looking forward to, was to become one of the saddest days in my life. As I was preparing to leave Bangalore I received a telegram from my mother to say that my father had died the previous day (9 September). I knew that he had been unwell for a long time, but in his kind and cheerful letters to me he had complained only of rheumatism or lumbago in his back. In fact he had cancer of the spine; my mother had deliberately kept this news to herself to save me worry, but in doing so had increased her own worries. Later in the war I did likewise and always tried to send good news back home, never mentioning such things as wounds, malaria or hepatitis.

Forty-two years later, in 1983, I returned to Bangalore with my wife to visit the old cantonment. The city had changed beyond all recognition and the site of the Officer Cadet School had been swept away in a mass of new buildings. We did, however, find the old garrison church, in a poor state of repair. It was obvious that the church needed a generous injection of money, for it was still used by a small congregation of the Anglican Church of Southern India.


## Meerut

I had a few days' leave before reporting for duty with 7/2nd Punjab Regiment in Meerut and I travelled to Delhi determined to see as much of northern India as possible. Fortunately, two good friends, both from Stonyhurst College, whom I had met in training with the Royal Scots, and who were also joining regiments near Delhi, came along with me: David Brigstock and Claud Wilson. (Tragically, Claud was killed in Singapore a few months later.) We stopped off in Agra to see the Taj Mahal, built by the Emperor Shah Jehan in memory of his wife Mumtaz, and we also visited the abandoned city of Fatepur Sikri. In Delhi we saw all the main sights, travelling everywhere in a *tonga* (ponycart). What impressed me most was Viceregal Lodge, guarded by the Viceroy's bodyguard in their resplendent uniforms.

Soon it was all over and, with considerable apprehension, I took the train to Meerut, famous for being the place where the Indian Mutiny of 1857 had its beginnings and also for being the home of the Meerut Tent Club, the most prestigious pigsticking club in India (hunting wild boar on horseback, armed only with a spear). As my train drew into the station I heard and saw a military band playing. Surely it could not be for me? My doubts were quickly dispelled when I discovered that they were playing off a military draft going to the Middle East. There was nobody there to meet me, so I hired a *tonga* and drove off to the military cantonment, where I reported

18

to the Adjutant. I was allocated a small bungalow, which I shared with another young officer. Our servants were numerous. We each had a personal bearer; in addition there was a *dhobi* (washerman), a *mali* (gardener – I never did find out what he actually did), and the sweeper who emptied our lavatory, which was commonly called a 'thunderbox'.

The officers' mess was situated in a large attractive bungalow about 200 yards away. On my first morning I was awakened by my bearer, Mohd Amin, at about 5.30 a.m. He brought me a mug of hot sweet tea and a banana, saying '*Sahib, bahadur ji jagao*', which literally translated means 'Mighty warrior arise'. Training usually started very early in the morning and carried through till afternoon with a long break for breakfast mid-morning. My first breakfast was memorable, for when approached by the Mess Havildar to ask what I wanted, I did not know what to say. I discovered that the other officers, who sat silently, were eating grilled peacock and *rumble tumble anda* (scrambled eggs), so opted for the same. I soon learnt that young officers never spoke at breakfast unless spoken to.

## Garrison Life

Life seemed strange at first, but I very soon settled in. The Battalion had only recently been formed as part of the war expansion and little did I know that it was to be my home for the next 4½ years. As in most Punjab regiments, which were recruited from a large area to the north of the Punjab States, there were two companies of Punjabi Mussulmans (Muslims who smoked, but abhorred pigs, and did not drink alcohol), one company of Sikhs (of Hindu origin, who did not cut their hair or shave, drank like fishes, but were forbidden to smoke), and one company of Dogras, recruited from the Himalayan foothills, who were orthodox Hindus (they worshipped the cow, but drank and smoked). It was all rather confusing.

## Our Soldiers

All three classes of soldier were magnificent in battle, and had a disciplinary record second to none. I looked upon them as loyal friends.

*Punjabi Mussulmans*
The Punjabi Mussulmans (PMs), who came from the Punjab (north), comprised approximately one half of the Battalion. They were almost 100% *zamindars* – that is, from farming stock – and were the most widely recruited class in the combatant units of the Indian Army. They had a great military tradition over many generations. I was struck by their quiet dignity and courteous manner.

*Sikhs*
The Sikhs, with their long hair, beards and distinctive turbans, were undoubtedly the most colourful of our soldiers. They complied strictly with the rules of their religion. Those rules that affected them personally were known as the 'five Ks':

- *kess* (hair and beard) – this they must never cut
- *kirpan* (small sword or dagger) – not carried in the military
- *karra* (bracelet) – worn on the wrist
- *kangha* (comb) – worn in the hair
- *kachar* (underpants) – always worn by the Sikhs, but not commonly worn by other Indians.

The Sikhs were dissenters from Hinduism in the sixteenth century and, unlike the Hindus, were monotheists. Their religious thinking was different from that of our Mussulmans and Dogras (Hindus). They had fought against the British in the two Sikh Wars of the nine-teenth century, which gave rise to a mutual respect between them and our soldiers. They had stood by us during the Indian Mutiny of 1857. Tall, handsome men of fine physique, they were truly a warrior race and distinguished themselves by their gallantry in battle. Their recruitment area was from the Punjab States north-west of Delhi.

*Dogras*
At one time the Dogras were classified as Punjabi Hindus for recruiting purposes. They came from in and around Jammu State in the foothills of the Himalayas to the north of the Punjab. Most came from distant villages, many miles from road or rail, and their recruit-ment was a very prolonged process. They were excellent soldiers and had that quiet composed demeanour that often comes from living in

close proximity to large mountains. They were by nature both generous and kind, but lacked the exuberance of the Sikhs.

None of the Indian warrant officers (*subedars* and *jemadars*) spoke English, nor, of course, did the men. My first and most important task was to become proficient in Urdu and I had lessons every evening from a *munshi sahib* (teacher). Urdu is a form of Hindustani; it incorporates many Persian and Arabic words and today is the official language of Pakistan. Learning Urdu was of paramount importance and I worked pretty hard at it. To my surprise I found that I could pick up the rudiments quite easily, but dealing with the requirements of daily life was only a start: I knew that, eventually, and maybe sooner rather than later, I must be able to command soldiers in battle.

Life was pleasant enough, with plenty to do. In the evenings we played games with our soldiers, rode horses and sometimes went shooting in the surrounding countryside for *chikoor* (partridge), pigeons and peafowl. Unsuspected storm clouds, however, lay ahead.

Attendance on various courses seemed obligatory. First came a physical training and gymnastic course at Lucknow, where I shared a bungalow in the grounds of the Lucknow Club with an extraordinary young officer who in the evenings covered himself with talcum powder and played his violin in the nude outside our bungalow. He was a talented man, with an honours degree at Cambridge, where he had also been a cricket blue. I heard later that he had been court-martialled and reduced to the ranks to serve in a British battalion and was eventually killed in Burma. The news saddened me, but he was quite unsuited to be a soldier. I was not a born gymnast and the course appeared to me to be of no earthly use. It was also unpleasant, particularly wrestling with Sikhs who had covered their bodies with mustard seed oil and were as slippery as eels; to add to the difficulties their knotted hair came loose and I was easily blinded by their greasy locks.

On 7 December 1941 we were stunned to hear the news of the Japanese surprise air attack on the American fleet at Pearl Harbor in Hawaii and of America's entry into the war. We in India were suddenly faced with a formidable adversary to the east. Two days later the Japanese invasion of Malaya began and on 10 December

21

we were shocked by the news that two of our greatest warships, the *Prince of Wales* and the *Repulse*, had been sunk by Japanese aircraft off the coast of Malaya. Hong Kong was captured on Christmas Day and a few weeks later Singapore and Malaya fell. Thousands of British and Indian troops were taken prisoner. In early 1942 the Japanese invaded Burma and approached the very borders of India. All this had a profound effect on us, for we realized that in a relatively short time we could be fighting to save India itself.

Japan's aim in going to war was to become the dominant power in the south-west Pacific and create a 'Greater East Asia co-prosperity sphere'. Burma was to be occupied to protect the flank of Japan's newly acquired territories and provide additional supplies of rice and oil. Burma could also be used as a springboard from which to invade India and, Japan hoped, incite an uprising against British rule.

The Battalion now moved from Meerut to Madras (2,000 miles south) by train in order to help garrison the city and port in the event of a possible Japanese move southwards in the Indian Ocean. I was promoted to Captain just after my 20th birthday. This was not promotion on merit; it just demonstrates that we were in part a schoolboy army and I found myself commanding a company. We all lived in large tented camps a few miles south of Madras, mostly in coconut plantations. Training had toughened up considerably.

I remember attending a troops' concert party where I saw fire-walking for the first time. This was particularly impressive as our chief clerk walked fully 20 feet over red-hot embers on his bare feet. There were the usual snake-charmers, but one revolting charmer put the head of a live snake in his mouth, bit it off and then threw the writhing body away.

In early April there were rumours that a Japanese fleet was moving south to attack Ceylon (now Sri Lanka), but that it might also attack Vizagapatam and Madras en route. The Brigade was ordered to move immediately to the port of Vizagapatam, some 450 miles north of Madras. This we did by road, leaving many vehicles stranded en route, thanks to the appallingly low standard of maintenance. I was appointed to be a liaison officer and was the first officer to arrive at Vizagapatam. There I contacted a splendid retired British naval officer who had installed himself in a lighthouse at the harbour and assumed operational command of the area. He had no staff and no communications, but he instructed me to tell my Brigadier that he had everything under control.

That evening Japanese Zero fighters attacked shipping in the harbour and sank two ships. A Gurkha battalion at the harbour was reprimanded by the Brigadier for not engaging the attacking aircraft with their own small arms. Next day the Gurkhas complied with the Brigadier's orders by shooting down our one and only aircraft, a general purpose Wapiti (top speed 135 mph); luckily the pilot was not killed. The Japanese threat passed and their fleet went on to Ceylon, where they sank two of our cruisers. Their naval aircraft were engaged by our Hurricane fighters based in Ceylon. There were severe losses on both sides, but the outcome was that the Japanese fleet never returned to the Indian Ocean, for they directed their future attention eastwards. Once again peace reigned and we all limped back to Madras along the same awful potholed road, all 450 miles of it.

## Snooty Ooty, the Queen of the Hill Stations

My battalion spent the whole of 1942 and the first half of 1943 training in Southern India, mainly around Madras. In late 1942 I was granted three weeks' leave and went to Ootacamund in the Nilgiri Hills of southern India. It was there that I spent some of my happiest times while I was in India.

Ootacamund, or Snooty Ooty as it was more popularly called, was founded by the British as a hill station at the end of the nineteenth century. It was probably one of the best-known hill stations in India. Today it is called by the Tamil name Utagamandalam, but most Indians continue to call it Ooty. There are still traces of its former grandeur, but for the most part it is only a shadow of its former self. Ooty lies amidst tea and coffee plantations at a height of approximately 5,000 feet. I had the good fortune to go on leave twice to Ooty during the war and on both occasions I stayed at a rather splendid house called Ratan Tata. Standing in attractive grounds, it had been handed over for the use of the Army by the Maharajah of Baroda.

There was a most attractive golf course, on which I tried to play a round every day. On one particular morning, playing very early, I was about to drive off on the fourth fairway when I suddenly became aware that something was radically wrong, not with my stance or my clubs but rather with the situation in general. I then heard a strange noise and, looking up the fairway saw, about 200 yards in front of me, a tigress, which came out of the bushes, clawed up some earth and then nonchalantly crossed the fairway and disappeared. This came as a complete surprise; I had no idea that there were tigers in this part of India and certainly not at a height of 7,000 ft. In 1983 I returned to Ooty with my wife and stayed in Ratan Tata for a few days. We visited the golf course and I was able to show her where I had seen the tiger. When I asked whether there were any tigers there today I was politely told that the last tiger had disappeared over 40 years ago.

Living not far from the golf course was a strange, primitive tribe of people called the Todas. They lived in simple, circular huts. Each hut had a doorway not higher than 2 feet and possibly not wider than 2 feet as well; these small doorways were there in order keep the tigers out! The most remarkable thing about the Todas was that they practised polyandry, a style of living in which a woman normally has several husbands. This is a very rare social custom that today is only generally practised among some Eskimos and Tibetans, but rarely elsewhere. On my return visit forty years later I asked where the Todas had gone, but nobody seemed to know; like the tigers they too had disappeared.

On one occasion I spent a day hunting with the Ootacamund foxhounds; we all charged backwards and forwards with a pack of foxhounds, chasing the local indigenous jackal. The foxhounds had originally been imported from England and had been bred at Ootacamund over the years. The Master and whips wore hunting-pink and everyone else was immaculately turned out, except for the handful of young officers (including me), who wore jodhpurs and tweed jackets. Like the tigers and the Todas, there are no foxhounds to be found in Ooty today.

On one of my visits to Ooty in 1943 I went with David Brigstock. He had been seriously wounded fighting the Japanese in Burma and his Ooty visit was to help him recuperate. There was a story going around that the Maharajah of Baroda had a harem approximately half a mile away out towards the golf course and that this harem was connected by an underground tunnel to Ratan Tata so that the old devil could get out there and divert himself in complete secrecy. Three of us decided to try and find this tunnel and then, if possible, go down it and reach the harem.

One sunny afternoon, after we had played golf all morning and then had our lunch, we decided to try and find out in which direction this tunnel ran. Our thinking was that it must have some air vents and it was on these vents that we concentrated our search. We used our golf clubs to poke around under the bushes in the garden and eventually our efforts were rewarded when one of us found an iron grille. With the aid of a torch we were able to look down and see what appeared to be an underground passage. We then followed the line of the passage and discovered further iron grilles, which were of course the air vents. Ratan Tata had underground cellars and in one of these we found a door let into the cellar wall, but painted over so that it would be difficult to find. There was a knob nearby that, when pressed, activated a release mechanism and the door slowly swung open to reveal a passageway beyond. All most exciting.

We decided to make our exploration of the tunnel a suitably grand occasion and after supper, having drunk two bottles of wine and suitably equipped with torches and gym shoes, we returned to the cellar. We drew lots for who should go first and the choice fell on me. The tunnel was much larger than we had imagined; we found that we could walk along it easily without stooping. After we had progressed some considerable distance a spot of light appeared at the far end of the tunnel, rather as if someone was holding up a rather weak torch. When we got closer we realized that it was light coming through the keyhole of a door some distance away. At this point I stupidly dropped my torch on the floor of the tunnel and we were enveloped by complete darkness. Amid considerable noise and clamour we made an ignominious retreat back to our starting point. This time I brought up the rear and I thought I was being chased by a horde of dervishes, for the noise we were making was increased by the echoes in the tunnel.

Arriving back in the cellar we took stock of ourselves and decided that we must make an immediate second attempt, but first of all another bottle of wine was necessary. Then we returned along the tunnel and reached the point where I had dropped my torch. It was lying, broken, on the floor. Light was still coming through the keyhole of what we now definitely knew was a door with a handle.

It was decided that I should be the one to open the door and go first into the room. In true Commando style I slowly turned the knob of the door and then jumped into the room, moving quickly to a flank. The room was nicely furnished, and there, thoroughly startled by our abrupt entrance, were a middle-aged man and a lady drinking whisky. They indignantly demanded to know who we were, but when I explained that we were looking for the Maharajah of Baroda's harem they both burst out laughing. They said that it had indeed been the Maharajah's harem, but that had been years ago. The man introduced himself as an Air Vice-Marshal on the staff of Lord Louis Mountbatten, Supreme Commander South East Asia, and then introduced his wife. Like us, they were on leave in Ootacamund and in fact were living with us in Ratan Tata but had been given the privilege of the old harem for their personal use. They offered us a drink, which we gratefully accepted. When we were about to leave they asked us why we had not turned on the electric light when we came down the passageway; it was in fact beautifully lit for the whole length of the tunnel, but we, silly idiots, had not discovered it.

During our 1983 stay at Ratan Tata we looked for the tunnel, but after over fifty years it was difficult to recognize the place and of the tunnel there seemed to be no trace. However, we met somebody who showed us an area that, so they said, did indeed lead to a passageway to the Maharajah's old harem.

*Chapter 2*

# THE ARAKAN

## Move to Chittagong and Arakan

The year 1943 saw a general turnaround for the better in the progress of the war in Europe, but in Burma the picture was different: the Japanese had deployed over a front of some 700 miles and threatened India itself. Our forces launched a limited offensive in the Arakan on the borders of India to clear the Japanese out of the Mayu Peninsula, but it failed. In October Lord Louis Mountbatten became Supreme Allied Commander South-East Asia and General Bill Slim took over command of the 14th Army.

Meanwhile, life in Madras continued on its course of humdrum training, but we were constantly hampered by an acute shortage of weapons, ammunition and transport. We lived in requisitioned houses and buildings in a somewhat rundown area on the outskirts of the city; this had a dampening effect on us and we wanted to move somewhere more active.

In March I had a welcome break: I was sent with my company to Rajahmundry, a large town some 300 miles up the coast from Madras. Gandhi's Congress Party was organizing protests against the war and calling for Independence, and our role was to support the police in the event of civil disturbances. The whole situation was most difficult. I was the only officer in the district and consequently at only 21 had to shoulder all military responsibility.

To add to the problems one of my young *sepoys* (soldier) murdered a senior NCO who was making homosexual advances to him. Much to my dismay the young soldier was court-martialled, sentenced to death and three months later was hanged in Madras prison. My sympathies were with him. Homosexuality was fairly common in India: not to the exclusion of marriage, but in addition

27

to it. In my experience the Sikhs were more prone to this than others. A story is told of how a maharajah from North India once visited Queen Victoria at Windsor Castle accompanied by two good-looking boys from his male harem. Queen Victoria is said to have been deeply touched by his compassion for young people. The soldiers' marching songs frequently had a homosexual theme. My own soldiers used to sing lustily a well known song called 'Zakhmi Dil', meaning 'Oh wounded heart'. A soloist would sing about a beautiful young boy who stood on the far bank of the Jhelum River; then came the chorus, 'Alas the river had no bridge and the river was too wide, was too deep and too strong'.

In September the Battalion embarked to sail to Chittagong (now in Bangladesh), the nearest port in East Bengal to the Arakan front. We were on the move at last and there was an air of great excitement. Our ship had previously been used to transport pilgrims to Jeddah en route to Mecca. She was rusty, dirty and ill-equipped. The voyage took us five days; on arrival in Chittagong we moved into a transit camp preparatory to moving to Ranchi in East Bengal to carry out intensive training and receive our new equipment, transport and weapons.

After our Ranchi training and refurbishment with new equipment, which included jeeps,* we made our way by train, trucks and on foot to the Arakan on the very border of Bengal and Burma. We encountered a late monsoon; the rains were particularly heavy and it required continuous work to keep the one poor road open for use by trucks and mules. Sometimes local coolies were used; they were dishonest, undernourished and dirty. The contractors possessed enough low cunning to exploit our difficulties and began a system of blackmail by overcharging and threatening to withdraw the labour unless we paid what they demanded.


## The Arakan

The Arakan is the area that divides upper Burma from Bengal (now Bangladesh). It is a place of densely forested hills interspersed, under

---

* US four-wheel-drive small vehicles, which could literally go anywhere.

the lower slopes, with rice fields and intersected by tidal creeks. On the hills the forest is impassable except by cutting one's way through it. The climate is typically tropical. The monsoon starts in May/June and lasts until September/October. During the monsoon period the rice fields can be 3 or 4 feet deep in water; the rain is almost unceasing and malaria is rife.

Following the monsoon the dry season lasts throughout the winter months from November onwards and then the banks (or 'bunds') between the paddy fields are high enough to restrict the free movement of vehicles. The climate changes at this time from torrential rain to hot burning sun during the day and bitterly cold early mornings, when the mist drifts in swathes between the jungle-covered hills over the myriad small rice-fields. I remember the Arakan for the mud of the rainy season, the choking dust of winter and the dank misty dawns, when the silence was shattered by the clatter of small arms fire or the thud of grenades and mortars.

The ground over which the Arakan battles were to be fought was an area of roughly only 10 miles square. The Mayu Range dominates the whole Mayu peninsula and has an unmade road running along the coastal area. The British plan was to push forward and clear the Mayu peninsula as far south as to command the mouth of the Naf River for sea supply and to secure the Maungdaw–Buthidaung road. The importance of this road was that it tunnelled through the Mayu Range. It had considerable tactical value: originally a railway line, it had two tunnels, which became a vital artery of supply for the Japanese in the Arakan battles.

The final march was over a distance of about 110 miles and took us five days. Few marches could have been worse. During the day the sun blazed down, interrupted by intermittent heavy showers. During the night it rained steadily. The surface of the road was of soft, wet, sticky clay, badly broken up by military vehicles. Our boots and legs were soon caked knee-high with mud and frequent halts had to be made to let everyone scrape and hack it off. This nightmare march ended in late September. We took up defensive positions in the foothills of the Mayu Range and became a part of 89 Infantry Brigade, which consisted of the 2nd Battalion of the King's Own Scottish Borderers and the 4th Battalion of the 8th Gurkha Rifles.*

* An outline of our Battalion organization is given in Chapter 5.

29

We entered the Arakan feeling fit and ready to face whatever lay ahead. Morale was good, but there were no officers with any operational experience and we knew very little about our potential enemy. Generally speaking we were inadequately trained in jungle warfare.

Little did we realize that we were all being subjected to a slow dehumanizing process, which became worse as this savage war went on. The Japanese harassed our positions at night, making us retaliate with small arms fire and mortars, but in the morning there were frequently no dead Japanese. Our CO, Robin Rouse, issued strict orders that this lack of fire discipline was to cease and I passed on his orders. Much to my surprise the next day my *Subedar*, Allah Dad, showed me three dead Japanese lying in a stream. He explained that he had purchased them from another unit on the other side of the Mayu Range for two bottles of rum. His idea was that when next there was fighting at night we would take the bodies out of the water, dry them in the sun and present them to the CO Sahib. Next night there was once again firing but no bodies and, according to plan, we produced our dead bodies, having first dried them out. The CO was delighted. This hoax, which was deceitful and in extremely bad taste, rebounded when later an intelligence report stated that the identification on our Japanese bodies showed that a particular unit had moved from one side of the Mayu Range to the other. I had to own up. I was left in no doubt as to what the CO thought.

Official casualty figures for the first six months of 1944 show that losses throughout South-East Asia Command in killed and wounded were 40,000, but wastage from sickness and diseases accounted for 282,000. The sickness rate in the Arakan was the highest. Before reaching the Arakan the CO addressed all ranks and said, among other things, 'Doh dushman hain. Ek Japani wallah hai; dusra machhe hai', which translated means: 'There are two enemies facing us: one is the Japanese and the other is the mosquito.' We took rigid steps to ensure that all ranks took an anti-malarial pill (mepacrine) daily and it was an offence not to do so. I had the misfortune to fall victim to a severe attack of malaria soon after arrival in the Arakan and put it down to not having taken the pill for long enough. I spent two weeks in a makeshift hospital within the Divisional area. This was my one and only attack of malaria in Burma, but I suffered periodic severe attacks for some years after the war was over.

Washing was often difficult and there was a great deal of ringworm. Another problem was the continual presence of blood-sucking leeches, which penetrated everywhere, even through the eyelets on our boots. There was no pain, but when we took off our socks we found them full of blood. Even the smallest leech could gorge enough blood to become five to six times its normal size. A doctor told me of a horrifying case in which a British soldier had a leech enter his penis: small wonder that we lived in dread of these creatures. For additional excitement one of our soldiers on patrol was killed by an enraged wild elephant, which seized his rifle in its trunk and beat him to death with it.

Towards the end of the year the 81st West African Division arrived. They caused our soldiers much amusement by marching through our positions barefoot and carrying their boots on their heads. Our Indian soldiers referred to them in good humour as *jungli wallahs*. It was said that the Africans were adept at jungle warfare and night fighting, but the reality was somewhat different, for they found themselves in a strange environment and were frightened of the dark. They attributed all noises heard at night to juju spirits. They were more frightened of the juju spirits than of the Japanese.


## The Embodiment of Leadership

The two officers who had the most direct influence on our destinies within the 7th Indian Division were General Bill Slim and General Frank Messervy.

*Uncle Bill*
There is no doubt that the confidence and morale of the 14th Army in Burma derived from the singular inspiration of General Bill Slim, or Uncle Bill as he was more popularly known. To Indian soldiers he was Cha Cha Slim Sahib, *cha-cha* being Hindustani for 'uncle'.

I never actually met Uncle Bill, either in Burma or afterwards, although I got to know his son John, now Viscount Slim, who was a regular officer in the Argyll and Sutherland Highlanders, when we were together in the Korean war in 1951.

Nevertheless, in the Burma war where land communications were notoriously bad, movement often only on foot and the total area of operations was vast, Uncle Bill's spirit of confidence permeated everywhere and to everyone. This was before helicopters were in use and front-line troops had no newspapers or radios. (Later in the war there was a brief news-sheet printed by South-East Asia Command (SEAC), which had a general distribution.) 'Uncle Bill' was the embodiment of leadership. How he achieved this I do not know, but three factors predominated: integrity, steadfast courage and, ultimately, success in battle.

Lord Louis Mountbatten, the Supreme Allied Commander South-East Asia, did visit us in the Arakan and I met him again in 1944 in Kohima. I was impressed by his handsome appearance and charm, plus the attendant aura of royalty, but it was Slim who left the more lasting impression.

Slim came to Burma in March 1942 to command a hotchpotch Burma Corps. Rangoon had just fallen to the Japanese and his arrival could hardly have been more unpropitious. Our troops were exhausted, with no chance of reinforcement or re-supply. Slim brought the survivors out to India and safety – still carrying their personal weapons. After a brief spell as a corps commander he was appointed to command the newly formed 14th Army in Burma.

Slim had fought in World War I at Gallipoli, where he was wounded, and also in Mesopotamia (Iraq). He then joined the Indian Army, became a Gurkha and later commanded the 7th Gurkha Rifles. Soon after the outbreak of World War II he commanded a Brigade in Eritrea (a former Italian colony on the Red Sea) and later the 10th Indian Division in Persia (Iran). At the time of the first battles in the Arakan he was a hardened and most experienced soldier with a deep understanding of British and Indian troops, able to speak both Urdu and Gurkhali fluently.

*General Frank Messervy*

General Frank Messervy, commonly known as General Frank, like Uncle Bill had served in World War I. He was an old Etonian with a great sense of humour. Being a brilliant horseman he joined Hodson's Horse, an elite cavalry regiment in the Indian Army. He served on the Western Front and took part in General Allenby's great cavalry sweep from Palestine into Turkey in 1918.

In the aftermath of World War I, when aide-de-camp to Lord Reading, he met Mountbatten, who was then ADC to the Prince of

Wales, and told him that the proper way to mount a polo pony was to run at it from behind, take a flying leap and vault up into the saddle, a trick that tickled Mountbatten's sense of humour, but which was beyond his agility.

Messervy also had the reputation of being an accomplished scholar. He became an instructor at the Indian Staff College in Quetta at the same time as Colonel Bernard Montgomery whom he insisted on referring to as 'His Royal Highness the Emperor of Ethiopia' whenever he appeared wearing a white cork pith-helmet as favoured by that monarch.

General Frank took over the command of the 7th Indian Division in the summer of 1943 at Ranchi; previously he had been with the 4th Indian Division and the 7th Armoured Division (the Desert Rats) in the Western Desert. The story of how he escaped capture by General Rommel's armoured forces when his headquarters was overrun, by taking off his badges of rank and impersonating an old soldier, caught the imagination of the troops. The 7th Indian Division had got a leader that it deserved – talented, humorous and inspiring.

I clearly remember General Frank addressing all officers of the Division in a battered old cinema in Ranchi just before we departed for the Arakan. It was nothing short of a call to war. It was brief, with flashes of humour and full of confidence. I found it exciting and uplifting, but at the same time it left me feeling apprehensive about the future.

## Peaches and Cream Sahib

Late in 1943 my Battalion found itself deployed in north-west Burma along the mountainous Mayu Ridge; there were no roads and no footpaths other than the tracks made by wild animals. The monsoon had only just ceased, but it had left behind good conditions for rapidly breeding leeches. It was under these difficult conditions that we faced the threat of attack from Japanese divisions some 15 miles to the south. Vigorous patrolling was the order of the day.

In early November a newly commissioned British officer arrived in the Battalion. To us hardy veterans of 21 years of age and 2 years'

33

commissioned service he looked extremely young and innocent. His name was Simon, and because of his rosy complexion he immediately earned the sobriquet of 'Peaches and Cream sahib', or PC for short. Soon after his arrival he was, like the rest of us, thrown into the deep end. He was ordered to take a strong reconnaissance patrol along the Mayu Ridge to a point from where he would be able to overlook a Japanese base just outside Buthidaung. The patrol's main task was to report on the general activity in the area; a secondary task was to kill at least one Japanese and bring back his insignia so that we could identify any new units in the area. In addition to PC the patrol consisted of six *sepoys* (Indian soldiers) and a *havildar* (sergeant). They were to carry rations for six days, to cover two days out, two days observing and two days back.

On the second day of their observation they saw two Japanese soldiers, carrying their personal weapons, come down to a small stream and begin fishing with little bamboo rods: not unlike our own coarse fishermen back in England, who sit out along the canal banks and waterways. PC decided that this was the best opportunity to kill at least one of them. He made a simple plan: he and two snipers would slowly, unobserved, work their way down towards the *chaung* and get into good firing positions.

So far so good. But then, to the amazement of his patrol, he explained that it was most unsporting to shoot unsuspecting Japanese soldiers who were engaged in a sporting enterprise, even though they were tough and dangerous enemies. He explained that he would crawl to a flank, position himself behind a small bush and, when all was ready, would stand up and shout 'Boo you bastards', while at the same time opening fire with his Sten gun.

The plan worked splendidly, except that PC's Sten gun jammed and the Japanese had time to hurl two hand grenades in his direction, seriously wounding him in one leg. The patrol killed the two Japanese and got the necessary identifications. Then came the long and arduous task of evacuating poor PC. He was eventually taken to a base hospital in India, where he had his injured leg amputated. After the war he had a successful career on the London Stock Exchange.

Afterwards, General Frank issued an Order of the Day to All Ranks, which read: 'Remember that the Japanese are not pheasants and you can shoot them on the ground.' This must have puzzled our Indian soldiers, and perhaps many a British soldier too.

It is vital to be able to maintain a sense of humour in war. It has been my good fortune to have spent my military service with soldiers who at the bleakest of times could discover some opportunity to laugh, and what is more were able to laugh at themselves. There is a story from World War I that the German General Staff became convinced that British troops could endure the winter hardships of the trenches better than their own soldiers. They concluded that one of the prime reasons for this was that the British had a better sense of humour, which helped to maintain their morale. In consequence they produced a pamphlet on how to develop a sense of humour. On one page there was a reproduction of one of Bairnsfather's famous cartoons showing Old Bill sitting in a devastated dug-out with one wall completely blown in by a shell. One of his chums comes along and, seeing Old Bill, asks: 'What made that hole?' Old Bill replies: 'Mice.' The German pamphlet has an explanatory footnote saying: 'It was not a mouse, it was a shell.'*

## 'Pimples'

In early January patrol activity increased along the whole Arakan front. There was a general feeling of optimism and there were rumours of a coming offensive by us. To add to our optimism the days were sunny and bright, and the nights cool. The monsoon was behind us and the dreaded leeches had disappeared to wherever leeches go in the dry season.

The only operation of any importance at the time was a Brigade plan to capture some high ground comprising three hillocks called 'Pimples', which had been occupied by the Japanese and had to be cleared before any further advance could be made. The King's Own Scottish Borderers (KOSB) put in a night attack, but met with heavy opposition and suffered a number of casualties.

My battalion was then ordered to make a further attack the following night with two companies coming under the command of the KOSB. I commanded one company and a friend of mine, 'Bundo'

---

* A copy of the original is in the Imperial War Museum.

Uwins, the other. At first it all seemed plain sailing, but on reaching our objective it was heavy going through thick scrub in the darkness. Suddenly the world erupted around us: the Japanese opened up with small arms fire and grenades, and to make things worse we came under heavy mortar fire. The night sky was lit by tracer bullets and Very light flares. For the first time I experienced the Japanese habit of shouting and chattering in battle.

When the first glimmers of dawn arrived Uwins and I tried to take stock of the situation, but almost immediately he was shot dead while standing beside me by a sniper concealed in a tree. He was shot through the heart and died immediately, falling backwards down the hillside. I instinctively did likewise. At first there was no trace of blood on Uwins; his eyes were open and I tried to talk to him. It was a little while before the truth sank in that he was dead. I too was hit, presumably by the same sniper. The official battalion history recounts: 'Major Shipster was shot in the throat, although not fatally.' The bullet passed through my shirt, cutting across my neck; there was no pain, just a lot of bleeding, which later necessitated my being evacuated to a field dressing station. In the meantime I was able to remain with my Company with a field dressing around my neck.

The sudden and totally unexpected death of 'Bundo' Uwins came as a great shock to me. It was particularly shocking as he was a close friend and it was my first experience of death in battle. He was the first officer in the battalion to be killed in the Arakan. While on 'Pimples' my Company had been in support of his Company. Now I found myself responsible for two Companies, not knowing where the Japanese were except that they were obviously on the high ground above us.

There was considerable activity going on away to our left and I presumed that this came from the area of the KOSB. No progress was going to be made by just staying where we were, so I decided to attempt to get up to the top of the ridge, taking one platoon with me. What had seemed so difficult during the night now proved to be comparatively easy and we got astride a small track running along the summit. We could hear movement along the track to our left and froze, weapons at the ready, but we were relieved and delighted to contact a patrol from the KOSB.

Later we were able to clear 'Pimples' of all remaining Japanese without much further trouble. When we were on the top of our objective and the early morning mist had cleared we could more fully appreciate what a commanding position the feature was, overlooking a wide area of disused paddy. Later in the morning, when the sun was up, I saw what I thought was a dead Japanese lying on his back in the open some 300 yards away. To my surprise he slowly raised his arm and then lowered it; much later I saw him do it again. How he came to be there I do not know; he was still alive, but obviously severely wounded. In any civilized war we would have sent a stretcher party carrying a Red Cross flag to bring him in, but if we had done so either he would have killed himself or any remaining Japanese in the area would have shot at us. By the early afternoon his arm movements had ceased. Later in the afternoon the carrier platoon (tracked armoured vehicles) of the KOSB came to recover our casualties, which totalled forty-one between ourselves and the KOSB.

It was on 'Pimples' that I saw dead Japanese at close quarters for the first time. They were usually covered with flies and their squat bodies, sallow complexions and shaven heads made them look particularly hideous. I also had the opportunity to explore the Japanese bunkers, which were extremely well dug and camouflaged. Among their abandoned equipment were letters and photographs of loved ones left behind in Japan. It made me realize that they were not unlike ourselves and that they had families too. For me it was an important stepping stone in gaining confidence. The experience stood me in good stead for what lay ahead.

Soon after the 'Pimples' operation the Japanese were to carry out a major offensive in the Arakan, code-named Operation Ha-Go. 'Pimples' became just another forgotten battle. If I thought of it at all I looked upon 'Pimples' as being relatively unimportant and its capture a pyrrhic victory. So many British, Indian and Japanese lives lost – for what? There must have been countless other 'Pimples'-like operations during the Burma war that now lie forgotten, but for me, for a very short space of time, it was important and my whole being.

It was not until 1996 that I read *The Official History of the War against Japan* and much to my surprise found that 'Pimples' merited a special mention as regards its tactical importance, for it covered the approach to a main feature called 'Able', which overlooked the Japanese defence along the Buthidaung road and was known to them as the 'Golden Gate'. This made me feel better about a place where we had a number of casualties, where I lost a good friend in the death of a brother officer and where I missed death myself by only a hair's breath.

In the early years after the war I hoped that I was unscathed by my experiences, but even now I still sometimes wake up shouting, after dreaming of Japanese encounters. There can be few things more frightening than close-quarter fighting in the dark against an enemy as ruthless as the Japanese.

## Ha-Go

On 4 February the Japanese 55th Division, commanded by General Tadashi Hanaya, carried out a general offensive code-named by them Ha-Go. They planned to then launch a second offensive on the central front in north Burma aimed at Imphal and Kohima some 250 miles away across mountainous and jungle-clad country. On 6 February our Divisional HQ was attacked, but the Divisional Commander, General Frank Messervy, and most of his staff managed to escape and set up an alternative HQ in a position known as the Admin Box. It was rumoured that the General got away in his pyjamas. For eighteen days the Japanese pressed home their attacks but finally lost the battle, leaving 8,000 dead as witnesses to their defeat. For the first time in the war we had met, held and decisively defeated a major Japanese attack. General Slim said it was 'a turning point of the Burma War'. Churchill sent a typically Churchillian message, which read: 'The Japanese have been challenged and beaten in jungle warfare; their boastfulness has received a salutary exposure . . .'.

Very early on 4 February our Battalion was ordered to move immediately to intercept Japanese who had infiltrated to our rear. I was awakened before sunrise by my radio operator telling me to report to the Commanding Officer, Colonel Robin Rouse, as soon as possible to receive some urgent orders. There was a brief Orders Group meeting, the gist of which was that Japanese forces were advancing across the whole of our divisional front and had infiltrated at many points. The Battalion was to be ready to move in two hours' time; every man was to have had, if possible, a mug of hot tea. There

**HA-GO OFFENSIVE**
**Arakan, Feb–Mar 1944**

xxxxxx *Approximate original Japanese front line*

Bawli Bazar

Goppe Bazar

*Goppe Pass*

*Kalapanzin R.*

Taung Bazar

Briasco
Bridge

Div Admin
Box

5 IND DIV

89
BDE

Sadana

Kwazon

Ngakyedauk

*Ngakyedauk
Pass*

Sinohbyin

114 BDE

9
BDE

33 BDE

Pyinshe
Kala

Letwedet

Naf R.

xxxxxx xxx xxxxxxx xxx xxxx

Buthidaung

xxxx

Dabrugyaung

W
E Road
Tunnels

DOI
COLUMN

SAKURA
COLUMN

Maungdaw

N

*Miles*

0  1  2  3  4  5

was no time to harbour anxieties, just get cracking – pack up, check weapons and ammunition, dismantle telephones, check radios, sort out maps and, most time-consuming of all, load up the mules.

The morning was no different from any other in the dry season. There was a mist with heavy dew, formed in the small hours of the morning and normally persisting for a few hours after sunrise unless cleared by wind. The noise made by the dew falling from the trees on to the dry undergrowth was loud enough to drown the sounds of footsteps, so that enemy movement in the early morning could be unheard as well as unseen.

During the morning I saw for the first time Japanese Zero fighter aircraft with their distinctive red circular markings depicting their national emblem of the Rising Sun. They flew approximately fifty sorties over the Divisional area. Later in the day we saw various groups of Japanese moving in the same directions as ourselves and the noise of both small arms and gun fire could be heard all around us. Perhaps the Japanese were just as confused as we were. One particular event sticks in my mind: when moving across a small ridge I was confronted by three Japanese at about 15 yards and I killed one of them with my Sten gun. I was surprised how easy it was and shocked that I felt no remorse: I might as well have been shooting rabbits at home.

On 5 February we received orders to move back to the area of our previous location, but while preparing to move we were heavily attacked from two sides, making any movement on our part impossible. We inflicted heavy casualties on the Japanese, who came at us in suicide rushes.

My recollections of the next 24 hours are very hazy. I remember Robin Rouse asking me to try and make physical contact with our Brigade HQ (Brigadier Crowther), as we had lost radio contact. What we particularly wanted was information on Japanese movements. I took with me a young soldier, Sepoy Mohad Amin, and with considerable misgivings set off in the direction of where I thought our Brigade HQ was. I eventually found Brigadier Crowther and a small group of staff officers in a ravine. Although I hardly knew the Brigadier he greeted me like a long-lost friend and gave me a mug of cold tea and a cold chapatti, which in those circumstances was a banquet. His instructions were that we should try to get back to our former positions and 'stay fast' come what may. The Japanese intentions appeared to be to get behind us and sever our line of communication. With the greatest difficulty and a certain measure of fear I managed to get back to Robin Rouse, who issued orders that, under cover of darkness, we would withdraw. What was to come was a nightmare, for we were all exhausted, hungry and disorientated. Sometime later in the early morning of 6 February I established my Company on a small hill feature with the aim of holding out there as long as possible. Along with other positions capable of all-round defence I termed it My Box.

The situation at the time was extremely chaotic and remained so for nearly two weeks, with Japanese units both in front of us and behind. I had lost radio communications with my Battalion HQ and only later found out that their signals centre had been destroyed. I had no idea what was going on, other than the fact that there were the sounds of battle all around us. I was wounded immediately after arriving in our new location by a mortar bomb, which landed almost on top of my slit trench. My wounds were in my back and some of the numerous fragments penetrated one of my lungs. To this day I have the fuse cap and many fragments in my back. After lying in a trench for three days I managed to emerge and lead a small reconnaissance patrol. Fortunately we met up with a unit from the KOSB. I was then taken to a first aid post consisting of a few camouflaged tents, where there was one doctor, some medical orderlies and a large number of wounded, whom I joined as a stretcher case. There were, of course, no helicopters to fly us out. We did, however, receive air drops of rations and medical supplies, including life-saving penicillin, but no blood plasma which was so urgently needed.

## Japanese Generals

According to Louis Allen, the Burma War historian, General Hanaya was a notorious bully. At the least provocation Hanaya had been known to slap the faces of middle-ranking officers in front of their men, and on rare occasions order junior officers to commit suicide, offering them the use of his own sword should they hesitate.

Not all Japanese generals were in the mould of Hanaya. The Army compassed a wide range of eccentrics. General 'Tokuta' Sukarai, who led one of the assault forces in operation Ha-Go, arrived in the Arakan wearing a long pearl necklace. He told surprised officers that they were his lucky charms. Later, at a regimental officers' mess dinner, 'Tokuta' insisted on doing a Chinese folk dance; he stripped naked, and during his dancing puffed away at lighted cigarettes stuffed up his nose and in the corners of his mouth. When the dance was ended the cigarettes were given to the nearest officers to smoke. Later Tokuta's striptease act became legendary throughout the entire Burma Army.

# Japanese Operation Order for Ha-Go

*Operation Order A57*
*55 Division Order 0530 hrs 1 February 1944. At Battle HQ*

1. The main force of the Division will take the offensive on night 3–4 February. Allotment of troops is given in Appendix attached. Troops will come under command as from 1200 hrs 2 February.

2. Air Force Group will give the Division close support as outlined in Appendix attached.

3. Sukarai Column will pierce the enemy's line on the left bank of the Kalapanzin River and penetrate into Taung Bazaar and destroy the enemy in the area. It will then attack the enemy on the right bank of the Mayu River and destroy them in the area north of Buthidaung. The minor units on the present front line will remain in position and detain the enemy on their front by deceptive demonstrations. A detachment must deal with the enemy in the area of Goppe Bazaar.

4. Doi Column will remain in present positions. When Sukarai Column advances on the right bank of the Kalapanzin River it will take the offensive by destroying the enemy's centres of command and throw his rear into confusion and close the coastal road.

5. The artillery will cooperate with Doi Column. It will place a party of all ranks under the command of Sukarai Column to make use of captured guns.

6. Divisional Signals will establish a Centre at my Battle HQ on 3 February. Wireless silence will be broken at 0400 hours on 4 February.

7. I will be at Battle HQ.

HANAYA Tadashi
Commander

*Comments*

a) The location of Battle HQ is given, but I have been unable to locate it on the map. It was probably near Buthidaung.

b) In addition to Sukarai Column (Comd. Maj. General Sukarai) and Doi Column (Comd. Col. Doi) four additional Columns are mentioned, but no details of their roles are given.

c) The emphasis on air operations was placed on trying to maintain air supremacy. This they were unable to do. Their air operations after Day 3 dwindled to virtually nothing.

d) General Hanaya, when a prisoner of war in Siam in 1945, partly attributed his failure to being confronted by a tank brigade. This was, of course, a gross exaggeration.

I finally reached a base hospital at Chittagong in West Bengal on the evening of 23 February, some sixteen days after being wounded. The first part of the journey was on a stretcher in an ambulance jeep, which took me and others to an improvised airstrip, from where C47 Dakota aircraft were evacuating large numbers of casualties to different hospitals in India. My filthy, bloodstained uniform had long since been removed and my only possession was my watch. As money was of no conceivable use in the jungle I did not even have a wallet. After reaching hospital and undergoing surgery, my first wish was to get hold of some washing and shaving kit, have a bath and a haircut. My trunk was at our depot in Meerut, but that was 2,000 miles away. I forgot about it and accepted its loss as being inevitable. Some months after the end of the war, and before I returned to England, my mother was greatly surprised when the trunk arrived at her flat in London, having been dispatched to England from Meerut. It contained mildewed uniforms, a smelly mosquito net and my photo albums and books, which were stuck together and only partially retrievable.

## Japanese Attack on the Main Dressing Station

I learned later that the Divisional Main Dressing Station (MDS) had been attacked on the night of 7–8 February and there were many casualties among the patients. The MDS was situated in the Divisional Admin Box and was only a short distance from my Company Box, approximately 3 miles. Its function was to treat less serious cases and act as a staging post for those more seriously wounded. Much of the battle noise that I had heard from 7 February onwards came from the Divisional Admin Box. If it had been possible to evacuate me by stretcher after being wounded in my Box on 6 February, that is where I would have landed up, and in all likelihood I might not have survived.

The Japanese attacked the MDS at about 7 p.m. on 7 February. On hearing the news a medical officer went to investigate and was immediately shot at, but managed to reach the Divisional Tactical HQ some 250 yards away, where he gave a report to General Frank Messervy. A rescue attempt was launched by the 2nd West Yorks but failed. Four doctors were shot, despite protesting that they were non-combatants, and many patients were shot or bayoneted in their beds, including three wounded officers. The Japanese took some thirty prisoners; their hands were tied behind their backs so tightly that many cried with pain. No food or water was allowed for 36 hours and there were no latrine arrangements. When, later, some of our tanks attacked, the prisoners were placed in the open to be shot at, and those that survived were later lined up and shot. Fortunately about thirty-six patients, including malaria cases, were situated some distance away and escaped the attention of the Japanese.

The Japanese remained in the area of the MDS for three days. It probably suited them, for it was dug in and protected. We, on the other hand, were reluctant to put in further attacks which might incur any chance of killing our own soldiers.

The following first-hand accounts of the attack on the MDS convey some idea of the ferocity and brutality of the Japanese attack. First, as told by an NCO in the Indian Army Medical Corps:

I, along with six other Indian soldiers, was captured and ordered to carry three wounded Japanese on stretchers to their main base in the Buthidoung Tunnels. The journey took us two days, and we then expected to be released. Instead we were lined up on the edge of a small ravine and shot. The bodies were then kicked into the ravine, where there were at least twenty other bodies decomposing. By some freak chance I found myself to be only slightly wounded, and after feigning death extricated myself and managed to get back and tell my story.

As told by a British Private of the Royal Army Medical Corps:

I was taken prisoner by four Japanese at about 3 a.m. I was taken before some officers, who interrogated me on my nationality, the kind of work I did and the strength of our forces. Then I was taken with others to a quiet corner by some Japanese, who relieved us of all our valuables, then tied our hands behind our backs, made us face an earth wall and by some means, which I think was jujitsu, dropped us from our own height on to our backsides – it was very painful. When we fell they kicked and cuffed us; this went on for about 20 minutes. After that we were taken away and tied up in pairs. They made us go to a place where the ground was wet and soggy and full of bramble thorns; the slightest move was agonising. When daylight came, some of the soldiers came and cracked us on the heads with the butts of their rifles. They released some Indian prisoners to dig a few trenches; I saw an opportunity to get my hands released and they granted my request to join in with digging trenches. Afterwards they used me as a shield on top of the trench when the tanks came to blast out the Japanese. They refused to give us water or any medical treatment. I volunteered to carry water for the prisoners but this was refused. Eventually, after a lot of persuasion, we managed to get two bottles of water between 20 of us at about 5 p.m. It was just getting dark when an officer told us to come and get treatment. They took us far down a *nullah* to a clearing where a stream was running. There they opened fire on us with their rifles, killing 17. They left us all for dead and evacuated the place. Next morning an officer from the Queen's Regiment came that way and saw that I was still alive and got a stretcher party and brought me to the hospital. Out of all the prisoners, only myself, an officer – Lieutenant Basu (Indian Medical Corps) – and a British Other Rank from the KOSB came out alive.

As far as I am aware the attack on the MDS was the worst atrocity carried out by the Japanese in the Burma War. Although it is well documented in Louis Allen's authoritative book *Burma: The Longest War*,* surprisingly few Burma veterans seem to know of it. I am certain that the attack was not deliberate in its intention. The Japanese blundered into the MDS, but, having done so, their behaviour was savagely cruel.

## A Disastrous Finale

By the end of February Operation Ha-Go had been defeated and the Japanese had suffered losses far exceeding our own. There was much cause for celebration, but it must be remembered that our success was ultimately achieved by superior forces and an enormous air effort.

The Japanese withdrew roughly to the line of the Buthidaung road from where they had advanced a month previously, while we were regrouping and easing forward preparatory to attacking the Buthidaung line, termed by the Japanese 'The Golden Fortress'.

From my bed in hospital at Chittagong I was desperate for news of any sort, but heard only rumours, some good, some bad. For some reason that I could never understand we had no access to a radio or a newspaper.

As a result of the very heavy casualties incurred during the February fighting the Battalion had been withdrawn from 89 Brigade in order to reorganize, re-equip and take what little rest it could. On 8 March orders were received to occupy a feature known as The Bulge on the west bank of the Kalapanzin River some two miles north of Buthidaung. The Bulge was a large area consisting of numerous small hills covered in thick undergrowth, in which it would have been an easy matter to conceal a whole brigade. This group of hills had formerly been held by the Japanese and their empty positions remained. No trouble was expected in the area and on the evening of 8 March the Battalion reported that it was in position and all was well.

* Louis Allen, *Burma: The Longest War 1941–45* (London: Dent, 1984).

46

On the night of 10–11 March the Japanese infiltrated and, unobserved, got onto a ridge immediately overlooking Battalion HQ. The position rapidly became critical and the CO was killed while personally leading an immediate counter-attack.

The ridge was eventually cleared with the aid of covering fire from Grant tanks of the 25th Dragoons. At the end of the battle the whole position was strewn with bodies, arms and equipment, including several medium machine guns. One dazed Japanese soldier who was taken prisoner said under interrogation that he was the only survivor of a suicide force of approximately 130 officers and men, who had been sent to reoccupy the feature and remain there until annihilated. It was impossible to make an estimate of the Japanese dead, for many were buried under the debris of broken bunkers and collapsed tunnels. Our own casualties were extremely heavy: nearly 150 killed and wounded. It was one of the toughest actions fought during the whole Arakan campaign.

This was the first occasion on which we had worked with tanks and many mistakes must have been made because of lack of training. Once our British officers had become casualties there was no one who could speak to the tank crews. Target recognition was achieved by pointing at a bunker with a flag on a pole. The tank commander would pick up the target and within seconds the 75 mm gun would open fire with an HE (high explosive) shell, followed by armour-piercing shot and machine-gun fire.

Something must have gone radically wrong for us to have suffered such heavy casualties. The job of the infantry should have been to give close-quarter protection to the tanks, which would then direct their fire unto the bunkers. I suspect that many of the infantry tried to attack the bunkers before they were neutralized. In the face of so much loss of life, and so much gallantry, it is inappropriate to speculate. Another puzzling question is: if The Bulge was important to the Japanese, why had they abandoned it and then returned? As the area was so large and covered in dense undergrowth perhaps the Japanese, unbeknown to us, were in occupation the whole time. The irony is that, having been allocated a peaceful area for occupation, the Battalion encountered a bloodbath.

## A Welcome Breather

I recovered from my wounds quickly and was discharged from hospital after three weeks and given a month's sick leave. It was a strange feeling, without family or friends readily available. 'Home', as I knew it, was my Battalion, and what remained of them were still in the Arakan. I was not in an adventurous frame of mind and decided to return to Ooty in the Nilgiri Hills, a place I knew and where the climate was good.

At Ooty I stayed at Ratan Tata, the officers' convalescent home that I knew well from a previous visit, played my usual poor golf and managed to get a couple of rides on horses belonging to the Mysore Lancers. Of course I had to get new clothing made, but Indian tailors (*durzis*) do this in seemingly a matter of hours; the rest I borrowed. In the cool sunny climate, 5,000 feet above sea level, I soon felt fit and ready to rejoin my Battalion. It is amazing how quickly the body heals itself when young. While I was in hospital it was suggested that my next posting might be to our Regimental Depot as an instructor. I have no doubt that those who made the suggestion were being kind, but all I wanted was to get back to my Battalion. The various battles and the appalling conditions frightened me as much as anyone else, but like many others I felt that I had to go back. Our soldiers, for whom I had a deep affection, had to soldier on, so why not I?

There were many differences between the British and Indian Armies but one fundamental difference was that in the Indian Army the officer's role was often paternal, and certainly not condescending. The relationship of the officer to his men was perforce closer. In 1943 I travelled with my Mussulman orderly Quadam Hussein from southern India to the Punjab, north of Delhi. Our train stopped at a small place called Dina, from where we walked 10 miles to his village, using a camel to carry our baggage. In his village I met his family and I stayed with a VCO (Indian Viceroy Commissioned Officer) who had retired from the Regiment some years ago. Many of our soldiers were recruited from the same districts, thereby creating almost a tribal feeling.

While I had been in hospital and on sick leave my Battalion had moved out of the Arakan preparatory to being switched to north-east India with the aim of reinforcing the Kohima front. New equipment had been received and reinforcements arrived from our Training Centre at Meerut. The move to the Kohima front was carried out by air, road and steamer up the Brahmaputra River, all part of a considerable logistic achievement in realigning our divisions for future operations and the relief of Kohima. The movement of troops and their equipment, including mules, from one front to another was the first use of air transport on a large scale in the Burma war. The aircraft used were C47s (Dakotas) of the United States Air Force (USAF). The Dakota later became the general 'workhorse' in Burma.

After leaving Ooty I went to Calcutta by train to rejoin the Battalion in East Bengal. I considered myself fortunate to find that I was to make the 400-mile river journey up the Brahmaputra River by paddle steamer to Gauhati and then 90 miles by road to Dimapur. For those of us going by boat it was a fascinating journey, taking some three days. The sunrises and sunsets over the vast river were spectacular. Occasionally we stopped for fresh supplies. At one particular stop a local man presented us with a very large number of turtle eggs, which made the most delicious *rumble tumble anda*. An interesting sight was the number of crocodiles of the gharial variety (long snouts) basking on the numerous sand banks. At the start of our journey we also saw some estuarine crocodiles (sea water), which grow to a very great length and are feared man-eaters. The worst recorded case concerning deaths from crocodiles took place in February 1945, when 900 Japanese soldiers were reported to have been killed when trying to escape from Ramree Island off the Arakan coast.* With hindsight I am glad that I never attempted to swim in the tidal rivers of the Arakan.

It was a great shock to return and find that Robin Rouse had been killed. He was recommended for a VC, but in the event was awarded an Immediate DSO, as was one of our company commanders. A newly joined Lieutenant just had sufficient time to get wounded and earn an MC before being evacuated. Of the officers, five had been killed and four wounded. I believe that we were the only Battalion throughout the Burma Campaign to receive three Immediate DSOs

---

* *Guinness Book of Records*, 1972 edition.

within a period of four weeks. Of the fourteen British officers who entered the Arakan only four remained. Of our Indian ranks 300 had been killed or wounded during the period January–March. Further bad news was that my wonderful second-in command, Subedar Allah Dad Khan, had been killed; he was a great friend and, with his experience, a 'father figure'.

*Chapter 3*

# FROM KOHIMA TO FINAL SURRENDER

## The Battle for Kohima

In mid-May in Dimapur I met our new Commanding Officer, Lieut. Col. Mainprise-King, for the first time. He was known in my regiment as 'Dahti Fahti', which means 'spick and span' in Punjabi, because of his usually immaculate appearance, complete with well-clipped moustache. The battle for Kohima had already been raging for a full three weeks and there appeared to be a stalemate in the vicious fighting. He told me that our original role had been as a reserve, but we had to send one company into Kohima to reinforce the 4/15th Punjab, who had suffered heavy casualties. Our Division had now taken over responsibility for all fighting within Kohima and along Kohima Ridge. The Colonel appreciated the fact that I had already been wounded twice and had only recently left hospital, but I had invaluable operational experience and he reluctantly wanted me to join my old Company and be ready to leave early the following morning. I suppose that in a way he was paying me a compliment, but it was not one that I cared for – to be considered a veteran at the age of 22.

I knew that there was heavy fighting going on in Kohima. But when, a few days earlier, I had been lazily steaming up the Brahmaputra River it had never entered my head that in a short while I would be involved in a battle that for its local intensity would exceed anything in the Arakan and would become the most renowned battle of the whole Burma War.

After the failure of their Arakan offensive the Japanese 15th Army attacked on the Central Burma front with the twin aims of seizing Imphal and the important hill station of Kohima to the north.

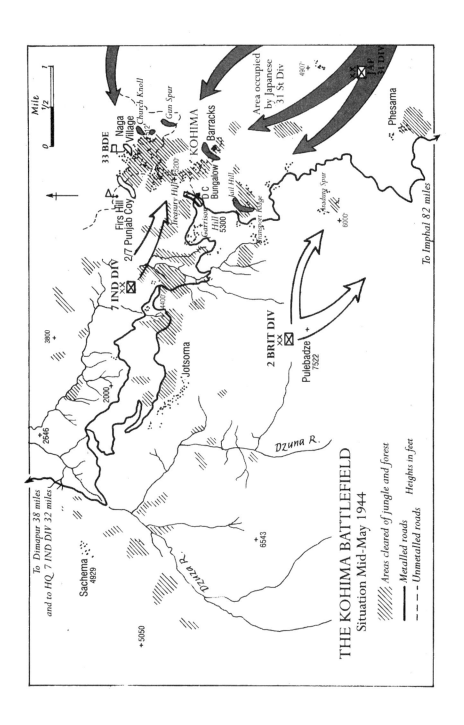

THE KOHIMA BATTLEFIELD
Situation Mid-May 1944

///// Areas cleared of jungle and forest

——— Metalled roads

– – – Unmetalled roads

Heights in feet

Mile
0    ½    1

To Dimapur 38 miles
and to HQ 7 IND DIV 32 miles

To Imphal 82 miles

Sachema
4929

+ 5050

+ 6543

Dzuna R.

Dzuza R.

+ 2646

+ 3800

+ 2000

4400'

Jotsoma

7 IND DIV
XX

2 BRIT DIV
XX

Pulebadze
7522 +

Anakay Spur

+ 6000'

Phesama

Area occupied
by Japanese
31 St Div

4907' +

JAP
31 DIV
XX

33 BDE

Naga
Village

Church Knoll

Gun Spur

5120

KOHIMA

Barracks

Firs Hill

2/7 Punjab Coy

Treasury Hill + 5200

D C
Bungalow

Jail Hill

Garrison
Hill
5300

Transport Ridge

52

Kohima, at an altitude of 5,000 ft, controlled the road to our supply bases in Dimapur.

Kohima lay at the neck of a pass through which ran the road from Dimapur to Imphal. During the hot weather in peacetime it was a welcome haven from the sweltering plains of India. It was not a town in the normal sense of the word; it was a ridge that ran alongside and sometimes astride the main road for a distance of about 3 miles. Looking from north to south the main features were: Naga village, the Treasury and Government offices, the District Commissioner's bungalow and tennis court, the hospital, the supply depot (DIS), the jail, garage, and workshops. There was also limited barrack accommodation for military units. From the top of the ridge there was a marvellous view of the surrounding hills, rolling away, seemingly endless, into the distance.

In peacetime when the weather was good Kohima had the atmosphere of an enchanted oasis, but instead of palm trees there were oaks, conifers and Australian gum trees. The built-up areas were a maze of small paths bordered by fuchsias, hibiscus, mimosa and geraniums. It was a gardener's paradise. There was a dark side too, for in the Naga hills were some of the most virulent mosquitoes in the world, spreading malaria. Typhus and jungle sores were also fairly common.

The local hill tribes of Nagas continued to occupy their villages even during the height of the fighting. Although forced to give help to the Japanese by providing food and acting as porters they remained intensely loyal to us. They were handsome, well-built people with golden brown skin. The men had pageboy haircuts and wore scarlet plaids of woollen cloth over their shoulders. To add to their colourful appearance they wore bead necklaces and hornbill feathers in their hair, in stark contrast to the horrors of war that surrounded them.

The Japanese intention was to advance from the Chindwin River across the Naga Hills, a distance of some 180 miles, and seize Kohima. This would cut the main supply route from Dimapur to Imphal. The 31st Division given this audacious task was commanded by an extremely tough and able commander, Lieut. General Sato. In the early stages of the advance some use was made of mechanised transport, where tracks permitted it, but the major part of the advance was to be carried out on foot and with mules.

Available livestock was to be requisitioned en route and driven forward behind the marching troops. Each soldier was to carry 15 days' supply of rations, consisting in the main of rice and tinned fish. It was hoped to obtain additional supplies on arrival at Kohima from the large amount of supplies that had been built up there. General Sato was of the firm belief that, with the road cut at Kohima, British resistance would crumble and a further advance might be possible to Dimapur, leading to the capture of our main supply base. Sato was unaware that after our Arakan victory we were moving two divisions to reinforce the central front.

Before leaving the Chindwin River General Sato assembled the officers of his divisional staff and drank a glass of saki with them, saying:

> I take this opportunity of making something quite clear. Miracles apart, every one of you is likely to lose his life. It isn't simply a question of the enemy's bullets. You must be prepared for death by starvation in these mountain fastnesses.

During the night of 3 April the first Japanese soldiers reached the road in the centre of Kohima. As dawn broke their presence was still undetected. Phase 1 of the battle had begun and the initial siege lasted over a period of approximately two weeks. The only troops in Kohima were an under-strength battalion of the Royal West Kents and a unit of the Assam Rifles; both units fought gallantly while being compressed into an ever-decreasing area. Relief finally arrived on 20 April when the siege was lifted. The liberators met 'little groups of grimy and bearded soldiers with bloodshot sleep-starved eyes. Unwashed they had fought and lived in their trenches for almost a fortnight with their boots on.'

In the early hours of 19 May I set off with my Company for Kohima not knowing what to expect. The monsoon had just broken and weeks of heavy rains lay ahead. It was to be a drive of about 45 miles along a twisting road, up and up through the Naga Hills. Well short of Kohima we got out and continued the last mile on foot. As we approached we could hear sporadic rifle and machine-gun fire, plus the louder bangs of artillery and mortars. We turned a corner in the road and suddenly the place came into view. I have never seen such devastation in my life. The former buildings were unrecognizable and the trees were gaunt skeletons, from which hung gaudy parachute canopies. In some places ammunition boxes swayed below the parachutes in the breeze. What hit me most was the dreadful stench of dead bodies, many of which had been lying there for over three weeks. One particularly unpleasant sight was a dead Japanese embedded in the soft tarmac of the road; as the days passed, his thin, wafer outline gradually disappeared.

My Company came under the command of the 4/15th Punjabis, and held a position to the north of Naga village. On my first night I shared a rain-sodden bunker with a young captain from the 1st Battalion The Queen's Regiment. I was saddened to hear, two days later, that he had been killed in an attack on a Japanese position.

The Japanese were dug in on a ridge just in front of us, known as Naga village ridge, from where they fired at any movement. During the next few days they carried out a number of night attacks and on one occasion penetrated into my position along a track that they had used previously. (I had learned in the Arakan that the Japanese frequently repeated their tactics using the same approach routes.) I had a young machine-gunner in a bunker covering this track and in the morning there were seven dead Japanese in front of his position. It must have been a terrifying experience for him and he rightly earned a Military Medal.

The 4/15th Punjabis were involved in some fairly heavy fighting further along the ridge in the area of Church Knoll on the main Kohima ridge and suffered a number of casualties in trying to move forward. Two officers, who only a few hours previously had invited me to have a drink with them after the success of the fighting, were killed.

Conditions were appalling, washing was impossible and hot food could only be distributed at night. To add to the difficulties there was the continual rain, which filled the bottom of our trenches. However, we didn't realize that the plight of the Japanese was far more desperate than ours and after a further two weeks they began to withdraw. They had suffered terrible casualties and had received no reinforcements or supplies. Their misery was compounded as their medical support was almost non-existent. General Sato took upon himself the responsibility for ordering his Division's withdrawal, which at times was little more than a rout. I have since read that General Sato was a more sensitive general than most others. The

Japanese High Command wanted to court-martial him, but did not do so, and he was eventually invalided out of the Army.

I don't think any of us realized that a Japanese withdrawal was imminent. It just seemed that one night they were there and the next morning they had gone. All that remained was the broken bunkers and trenches containing the unburied dead, discarded clothing, ammunition and other refuse of war. The Japanese suffered a crushing defeat at Kohima, but it had also cost us dearly. It was the furthest point into India that the Japanese ever reached and it marked the end of their invasion plans.

Relative to the very small size of the battlefield, the casualties on both sides were higher than in any other battle in the Burma War. British and Indian casualties amounted to 4,064 (killed and wounded) and Japanese 5,764, making a total of nearly 10,000.[*] Today there is a large cemetery at Kohima for British soldiers, with a prominent memorial that bears the moving inscription,

> 'When you go home
> tell them of us and say
> for your tomorrow
> we gave our today'.

There is also a memorial to all Indian soldiers who died in the battle, but there is no Japanese memorial other than a plaque in the local Catholic church.

After the battle was over Lord Louis Mountbatten visited the battlefields and decorated those of us who had earned 'immediate' awards in the Arakan. There was a small parade held on what remained of a local football field. Lord Louis had some kind and cheery words for everyone and remarked to my CO that he thought I was too young to be receiving a DSO.

The monsoon had already arrived in all its fury, but Lord Louis issued his well-known order 'Gentlemen, there will be no monsoon this year': by this he meant that there was to be no respite for us or for the Japanese, who were to be chased and harried despite the rains. The majority of the Battalion was not called upon to take part in the immediate pursuit, but was given some rest in the not too

* Louis Allen, *Burma: The Longest War 1941–45* (London: Dent, 1984).

extravagant comfort of Kohima. However, my Company got no rest, for in mid-June they joined a Brigade column, tasked with pursuing the Japanese to a place called Ukhrul. I remained with the Battalion in Kohima. I think Dahti Fahti thought that I had had enough. I spent only a short time in action at Kohima, but nevertheless I am proud to say that I commanded a Company in a forward position there, in what was a critical battle.

What did the tremendous events both in the Arakan and at Kohima mean to me? First and foremost I appreciated being with good men, whatever the colour of their skin, and whatever their religion. We had been put to the test and, I hope, not found wanting. We had proved our loyalty to each other and had been able to reap the rich rewards that this brings. None of us was blessed by any special star; we were all just ordinary people, who reacted to the environment in which we found ourselves.

I learnt to respect the dead, but did not mourn for them. Few of us did. This may seem insensitive, but it was essential for our own mental well-being. Having witnessed on so many occasions the casualness of death and the indiscriminate nature of its selection regardless of race, creed or colour, I am of the opinion that if there be a God he must be a God for all mankind. At Kohima it was not always possible to sort out the corpses. Bodies were buried together; there was no other way.

At school I had never been averse to religion, nor did I resent the daily services in the college chapel and religious instruction – in fact I enjoyed a great deal of it – but I am sad to admit that in the devastation and awfulness of Burma I cannot remember ever offering a prayer. I relied for comfort on the support of my own soldiers and in a practical sense on my map, compass and personal weapon. I have continued throughout my life to harbour both periodic doubts and guilt concerning religion.

I had thought that I would like to go back and see Kohima, but it is in Naga territory, which has recently been the scene of considerable unrest and it is very difficult to get permission from the Indian Government to enter. However, in 1987 when on holiday in India I did have the chance to go to Kohima, for our son was working in the High Commission in Delhi and could obtain the necessary permit. I turned the opportunity down; when it came to it, I did not think I could face Kohima again.

## Pursuit of the Japanese 31st Division*

The Japanese encountered appalling conditions during their withdrawal from Kohima at the height of the monsoon. They had reached Kohima on 3 April. In 20 days they had marched from the Chindwin River some 180 miles across the grain of the country and over endless ridges up to 8,000 ft above sea level: an epic march by any standards.

Now the remnants were returning ten weeks later, along the same tracks, depleted in strength, short of rations and with many wounded and sick. My Company, now commanded by Robin Rowland, was detached to join 33 Brigade, who were tasked with advancing eastwards along the main track to the village of Ukhrul, where the Japanese had a supply base. The Brigade had with them: 1 Queen's, who were considerably under strength; the 41st Gurkha Rifles; one battery of mountain guns; one company of Royal Engineers; and a detachment from a field ambulance unit, including a mobile surgical team. All movement was to be on foot and by mules, of which there was an amazing total of 1,760. The Brigade began concentrating on 23 June.

The view from the concentration area 15 miles south of Kohima at a height of some 4,000 ft was impressive. In the foreground green grassy slopes, as round and smooth as the South Downs in England, ran down to a river. A narrow red track wound steeply up a shoulder, losing itself in the dense forest covering the slopes of the mountains that towered overhead, a formidable cloud-topped barrier. The monsoon was at its height and storms of rain and cloud lashed the mountain tops; swollen by flood water, the rivers in the narrow valleys roared and frothed along their rocky beds. The violence of the monsoon was tempered by the precipitous heights and by the periods of sunshine that succeeded periods of rain throughout the day.

In the first stages of the march there was abundant evidence of the fierce struggle that had taken place along the track leading east. Dead Japanese and pack animals lay, stiff and ungainly, at the side

* This section is based on an account that I edited soon after the war was over.

58

of the track, in sheltered nooks in the hills and in battered enemy defensive positions. Equipment lay everywhere: water bottles, rifles and ammunition.

On 27 June the Brigade forded and swam the swollen torrent of a river. The crossing was difficult, for the river was spanned only by a narrow, railless bridge, 2 feet wide. Mules lost their balance, falling with a splash into the river, and were whisked away downstream until fielded by a line of soldiers in a shallow pool below.

Next day the column climbed steadily up into the clouds. A brush with a Japanese patrol resulted in ten Japanese casualties. The path ran ever upwards, becoming steeper, winding along the sides of deep valleys packed with decaying vegetation. The difficulties of crossing this country to reach Ukhrul, which lay some 80 miles away, were immense. Every foot of progress had to be hacked out of trailing vines, creepers and spongy-leaved bushes. Giant teak trees, rising through the dense undergrowth, shut out the light. The column marched slowly and steadily through the dim twilight under a thick canopy of green. No sound broke the silence other than the patter of raindrops, the subdued creaking of leather on metal and the heavy breathing of men too short of breath to speak. No birds sang; only leeches looked expectantly towards the living, sweating bodies. Torrential rain fell periodically; mist swathed and swirled in the valleys and around the towering peaks. In the bottom of the valleys swollen streams raged unabated, the noise of which could be heard thousands of feet above.

The Gurkhas attempted to cross a mountain range during moonlight and in the darkness twelve mules fell over the side of the hill. Six of these were never seen again, three were killed, one was retrieved from a tree in which it had been caught, and the other two were found grazing, their saddles smashed and loads scattered, 600 feet lower down.

Near Ukhrul the first real signs of the destruction wrought were seen. A fighter bomber strike had evidently caught a Japanese column moving up the track. The road was thick with dead bodies and littered with arms and equipment. Cautious progress was made through deserted camps of shelters constructed from leaves, and concealed strong points, probably capable of accommodating several hundreds. Unburied dead lay everywhere. Many were unwounded, some fat and well-looking, some emaciated skeletons – typhus, that scourge of armies, had done its work.

Ukhrul was captured against only light resistance amidst rumours that thousands of Japanese were dying in their efforts to reach the Chindwin River. The Brigade pressed on beyond Ukhrul. The rigours of the march had put a great strain on men and mules, most of whom were tired, weak and sick. The health of the Brigade was beginning to deteriorate rapidly and 1 Queen's were almost too weak to fight. The Gurkhas, with their amazing stamina, still remained remarkably fit. The mules were also in a poor state, for disease was rife among them and a number had died. Plans had been based on reaching Ukhrul and little margin remained. Many men were too weak to digest or retain their food and chronic diarrhoea was rife. For days on end many officers and men lived on a diet of rum and hot tinned milk, which was all they could manage.

From Ukhrul a track had been used before the rains as a main supply route by the Japanese. This narrow road wound along hillsides, dropped into valleys and climbed steeply up through forests. Never wider than a single vehicle, it had been transformed by the rain into a glissade of mud. Bridges were washed away and under the weight of abandoned Japanese vehicles the road collapsed in places in a slither of mud and shale down the hillsides. Everywhere the ravages of disease and starvation were apparent. From the large jungle camps lining the road, from *nullahs* and valleys lived in by the Japanese, rose the stench of putrefaction. At the side of the road or fallen down the hillside lay vehicles, the drivers dead at the wheel or lying beside their vehicles. Embedded in the foot-deep mud of the road were dead Japanese and the carcasses of mules worked to death in the frantic endeavour to escape. Equipment lay everywhere as evidence of a rout.

Despite all this the Japanese rearguard still held successive positions, each of which required two to three days to clear because of the difficulties of the terrain. Heavy mist and rain prevented air action, and along numerous jungle paths the sick and battered remnants of General Sato's 31st Division struggled painfully southwards.

On 16 July it was decided that the task allotted had been accomplished. Nothing further was to be gained by pursuit and 33 Brigade group was withdrawn to rest and reorganize at Kohima.

## Goodbye to Kohima and Pursuit to the Irrawaddy

After the bloody battle of Kohima, which ended in the early summer of 1944 with a complete defeat of the Japanese 31st Division, we all enjoyed a much-deserved rest. We were of course kept fairly busy, getting supplied with new equipment and absorbing reinforcements. I managed to get away on a short spell of leave to Calcutta in Bengal. Bengal (now a part of Bangladesh) was at this time suffering from a disastrous famine because the rice crop had failed. According to Indian Government official statistics over 3 million people died of starvation during three years of famine. This calamity was hushed up and I only learned about it after the war.

I went to Calcutta by train from Dimapur and stayed in a large hotel, requisitioned for officers on leave, in an area known as Chowringhee in the centre of the city. It was strange to move from the devastation of Kohima to the bustling activities of the largest city in India. My most vivid memories are of going to two race meetings and, much to my delight, having two good wins. I also ate well, which was a welcome change after our recent sparse diet. I took the opportunity to do some much-needed personal shopping. For companionship there were a number of young officers from the Burma front, some of whom I knew, but one did not have to know anyone to make friends in a wartime city.

What made life so very different when on leave was the total lack of female companionship. The reasons for this were varied and understandable. Most of us had no family or friends living in India; the few that did soon discovered that many wives had returned to England after the outbreak of war. Others had gone to the sanctuary of obscure hill stations if the head of the household had joined one of the Services. In wartime Britain there were thousands of women in the Armed Forces: in India there were only a few British nurses and a sprinkling of welfare workers.

In the 5½ years that I was overseas I hardly ever entered a private house, British or Indian; our social habitat was the clubs and messes. I had a great deal of sympathy for the problems of British other ranks in India.

I returned to Kohima refreshed, but after a very short time felt that I had never been away. In mid-December the 7th Indian Division

61

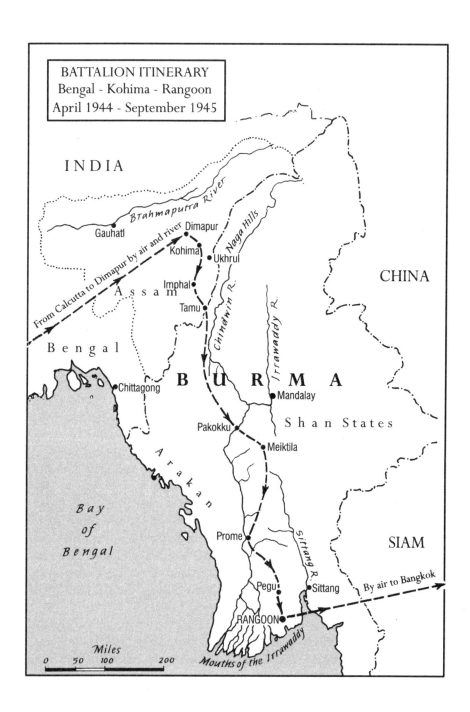

BATTALION ITINERARY
Bengal - Kohima - Rangoon
April 1944 - September 1945

INDIA

Brahmaputra River

Gauhati

Dimapur

Kohima

Ukhrul

Naga Hills

From Calcutta to Dimapur by air and river

Imphal

Assam

Tamu

Chindwin R.

Irrawaddy R.

CHINA

Bengal

Chittagong

BURMA

Mandalay

Pakokku

Shan States

Meiktila

Arakan

Bay
of
Bengal

Prome

Sittang R.

SIAM

Pegu

Sittang

By air to Bangkok

RANGOON

Miles

0    50   100        200

Mouths of the Irrawaddy

began moving in pursuit of the Japanese towards the Irrawaddy River. New roads had been constructed into Burma and the first part of our journey, 200 miles to Tamu, was completed in trucks. We then started operating in independent company groups giving protection to the left flank of the Division. This was an exhilarating time, for the weather was good, morale was high and we were heading in the right direction. I felt fit, but, like many others, was plagued with deep ulcerous jungle sores on my legs, which even when kept clean and treated with sulphanilamide powder (then a brand new treatment) were difficult to get rid of. The scars remained for many years. I believe that the causes of these ulcers was a lack of vitamin C, a generally poor diet and infection getting into cuts and abrasions.

Every evening we would take shelter in some relatively pleasant area, often near a small stream or river. Invariably just before the sun went down we would hear the unmistakable cry of the 'Fuck U' bird. Starting with a robust cry of 'Fuck U' it would continue its repetitious performance in diminuendo until the final cry just faded away in the evening air. The bird was always heard but never seen. One evening after the CO's conference had been continuously interrupted by this wretched bird, he announced that he would award a prize of 15 rupees (about £1) to any soldier who could provide firm identification of our tormentor. Returning to my Company I announced that the CO wanted an identification of the 'Fuck U' bird and that there was to be a good reward for this information. This news aroused considerable enthusiasm amongst our soldiers, for they had a child-like fascination for all games and competitions. No sooner had I stopped talking then the wretched 'Fuck U' bird started up. The soldiers immediately started scurrying about in the surrounding undergrowth while at the same time looking up at the trees, but with no immediate success.

After some time a very young and very shy soldier came up to me and said, 'I got him, Sahib.'

I said, '*Shabosh* [well done], but where is the "Fuck U" bird?'

The soldier replied that it was no bird, but rather a very large lizard, which produced a strange noise from the dewlaps under its throat, and he had been rather frightened by it! The soldier got his reward and so ended this delightful little mystery, which had kept us amused on so many evenings.

During the coming operations we were the Divisional reconnaissance regiment and companies moved and operated independently; this gave me great freedom. I had to plan my routes and radio for resupply from the air, which was sometimes tricky, as our demands had to be sent 48 hours in advance. Whenever we received rations, we also had to receive fodder for the mules – and of course we had to have spare mules to carry the fodder for the other mules, and so on *ad infinitum*. Rations for Indian troops were basic but very sustaining. They consisted of tinned milk, tea, sugar, flour for making chapattis, dhal (which is a sort of dried pea), and spices. Occasionally we got fresh vegetables and tinned fish, but there was no tinned meat thanks to the different customs of Hindus and Muslims in slaughtering animals. I ate the same food as my soldiers.

We passed a lot of abandoned Japanese equipment and on several occasions the emaciated corpses of Japanese soldiers who had died of illness or starvation during the retreat. It was only when we reached Tamu that we more fully appreciated the extent of the Japanese defeat; there were hundreds of abandoned vehicles in the area. The march from Tamu to Pakokku was over a distance of 325 miles across extremely difficult terrain; this we did on our own flat feet. Our only real excitement came when we ran into a Japanese ambush and temporarily lost most of our mules, including the one carrying my vital rear-link radio set. We had a small number of casualties, whom we were able to evacuate in light aircraft after clearing a landing strip. I even received letters from home in an airdrop, including some golf balls that my dear mother had sent me. So useful! Sadly I had to throw them away. Later I remembered that some months previously I had written home to say that it was impossible to buy golf balls in India.

At the end of one particularly exhausting day we stopped before nightfall to prepare the evening meal of the usual chapattis and dhal, washed down by a mug of hot sweet tea. The tea tasted especially good. After I had eaten, I walked up a small stream, which was the source of our water supply. Much to my surprise I found the rotting carcass of an elephant lying in a small pool. It certainly had not died as a result of any military activity and I can only presume that its death was from natural causes; but rotting elephant flesh certainly gave the tea that little bit of *je ne sais quoi*.

It may seem incredible now, but at the time I considered that leading a company of soldiers and mules on an arduous march into enemy-held country was a perfectly natural thing to do. None of my soldiers spoke a single word of English and there was no other British officer with whom I could discuss things should the need arise. Throughout the whole period of this operation the only time that I spoke English was when I spoke on my rear-link radio. Our speed of advance was very much governed by our mules, which had to be watered and fed. There were very few villages near our route and it was our policy to avoid all local contact if possible; it was well known that the Japanese had terrorized local people to give them any information concerning our forces, on pain of death if they didn't comply.

Our day started before sunrise with a mess tin of hot sweet tea and a chapatti, followed by the feeding and loading of the mules; this was always a tedious business, for they resented being loaded and delighted in kicking some unfortunate soldier or, better still, trying to bolt. On this march silence was the golden rule and the only noise to be heard was the movement of the mules and the chafing of the harness. In the evening we aimed to halt well before it was dark in order to look after our mules and feed ourselves. Finally, defensive positions had to be dug and manned, and then there was always quite a lot of signals traffic to be dealt with. As the weather was fine and clear the skies at night provided a marvellous, twinkling picture of the firmament. I had learned the names of the most prominent stars for navigational purposes, but I was made only too well aware of how little I did know. When I looked at the stars I am sure I never thought about the war, but rather about what was out in space. I always slept well, but awoke immediately at any unusual sound.

The final stages of the advance to Pakokku developed into an exciting race as to who would reach it first: us or other units in our Brigade. We encountered less opposition than them and arrived first by a short margin of 12 hours on 15 February. Soon after arriving at Pakokku Dahti Fahti asked me to accompany a Royal Marine sergeant, who was a member of an organization that I had previously never heard of, called RM Small Operation Group (SOG), who were equipped with collapsible canoes. Our purpose was to find out whether there were any Japanese stragglers on a small island in the Irrawaddy who might prejudice a future crossing.

We set out at dawn in a small canoe, taking only our personal weapons with us. Everything was very quiet and we beached our canoe and walked up a small path through some tall rushes. Suddenly I found myself in a small clearing facing about a dozen Japanese soldiers sitting eating rice. I fired my Sten gun, but one of the Japanese threw a grenade, which burst in front of me, and shrapnel penetrated both my thighs. The sergeant covered me by firing his own Sten gun and I was able to get back to the canoe before collapsing. Everything felt numb; I was bleeding badly and my trousers were ripped to pieces. The Sergeant managed to lug me into the canoe and get me back. The first thing that I asked our Battalion doctor was whether I had lost my private parts. He replied that everything was OK, but that I would have to be evacuated to India for surgery. Luckily, there were a number of light aircraft on a small strip nearby and within an hour I was in a casualty clearing station (CCS), given a shot of morphia and flown back to a base hospital at Comilla in East Bengal.

I woke up in an Indian general hospital, having been mistaken for an Indian soldier. Presumably the mistake occurred because, on arrival, I was sedated and unconscious; I was wearing no badges of rank and looked tanned and dirty. One thing that troubled me a great deal was that I forgot the name of the Royal Marines sergeant and I was never able to contact him again. He had saved my life and I was never able to thank him. The Japanese must have thought that we were part of a larger force and they were concerned only with trying to escape. If they had chased us, they would have found that we were sitting ducks.

I was in hospital in Comilla for about four weeks. Once again I had arrived with no possessions other than my wristwatch and had to re-equip myself. The wounds were not serious, but they took a long time to heal. One of the problems was that, although the doctors had removed the grenade fragments, there was a certain amount of cloth from my trousers in my legs, which did not show up on the X-ray photos. In later years both my legs gave me a lot of trouble as bits of metal worked their way to the surface. After about two weeks I was beginning to walk, but it was slow and painful. At the end of March I had to be examined by a medical board, which downgraded me and sent me to a convalescent centre in the Himalayas at Darjeeling. The board further recommended that I should have three months' sick leave; this seemed somewhat excessive, but perhaps they were just being kind.

While in hospital in Comilla I and some other officers, when asked what religion we were, replied 'Quaker'. This was in protest at what seemed to be needless and repetitive documentation. Three weeks later, when I was the only pseudo-Quaker in the hospital, I was told by the ward sister to report to the administrative officer, who asked me if I really was a Quaker. I had to admit that I was not. He explained that he had received a request from Statistics Branch at GHQ Delhi to investigate how it was that 100 per cent of officer casualties on the Central Burma Front on a particular date were Quakers, when Quakers comprised only 1 per cent of the Army. I had to apologize on behalf of us all.

I was delighted to go to Darjeeling. It was one of the most popular hill stations in India, being some 6,500 feet up in the Himalayas. It had been a convalescent centre for British soldiers since the mid-1800s. I took the train first to Calcutta, then to Silguri in the Himalayan foothills, and changed onto a 2-foot gauge railway known as the 'toy train', which climbs up to Darjeeling by means of various loops and switchbacks through picturesque tea plantations. The weather was perfect. Darjeeling seemed a wonderful haven of peace with its magnificent views of the snow-capped Himalayas. From a nearby vantage point one could see two of the highest mountains in the world, Everest (29,078 feet) and Kanchenjunga (28,208 feet). The local people were both intriguing and attractive; they were a mixture of Nepalese, Sikkimese and Bhutanese.

## Walking in the Himalayas and Tibet

While I was in the convalescent centre in Darjeeling I became friendly with a young naval officer called Peter (I am ashamed to admit that his surname has escaped me). We decided that, if possible, we would walk into Sikkim State, across the Himalayas into Tibet, and along the Tibetan trade route to Gyangze en route to Lhasa. It was now mid-April and the weather was perfect for walking, with the snow line at about 13,000 feet. What was more important, I felt fit again. The difficulty was to get permission to enter Tibet, as it was a 'forbidden' country. Luckily, my friend was a botanist and after a great deal of persuasion we managed to get a permit from the Tibetan Agent in Darjeeling to enter Tibet in the course of botanical research. Additional good luck was that the Indian post and telegraph authorities offered us two ponies to take the mail through to Gyangze, where there was a small Indian trading post, a journey of about 200 miles from Darjeeling. The station staff officer offered us a supply of hard rations, and finally, with the help of local people, we hired some Nepalese porters and an ex-Gurkha soldier, who was to be our cook and general factotum. His name was Kinsok; he was a splendid cheerful man, who had been on a Mount Everest expedition and could understand Tibetan. I was able to speak to him in Urdu.

We set off in high spirits, first descending to the subtropical Teesta River valley, where we collected a large number of parasite orchids growing on the forest trees. We then climbed up some 5000 feet to Gangtok, the capital of Sikkim State, where we stayed as guests of the Resident Adviser to the Maharajah. We had been intending to stay in a local guest house, but the Resident offered us the hospitality of his own house. He was a kind but eccentric man who, like me, was an old Marlburian. His two main ambitions were to introduce trout fishing to some mountain lakes and to construct a good cricket pitch in Gangtok. It all seemed a thousand light years away from the battlefields of Burma.

Our daily routine was relatively easy. We rose early; after breakfast, which usually consisted of tea, tinned bacon and biscuits, we started walking. Kinsok, the porters and the mules were accompanying us. We stayed in dak-bungalows (*dak* is Hindustani for mail). These were wooden travellers' huts, usually spaced between 13 and 15 miles apart. On arrival in the early afternoon we had our main meal – usually curried dhal and rice, followed by tinned fruit or tinned cheese. We had a light meal in the evening. To vary the diet we carried an assortment of tinned food; there were no trading posts and it was impossible to purchase any provisions.

In this particular area of the Himalayas the foothills in April are covered with a mass of varied coloured rhododendrons; there are reported to be some 400 different species in Sikkim. At the lower altitudes there are many different exotic butterflies, and possibly Sikkim has more varieties than elsewhere, for 600 different species have been recorded. I have never seen anything more beautiful than Sikkim in spring. The only wildlife we saw were the occasional exotically plumed Chinese pheasants, and once we saw a *bharal* (a large horned mountain goat) There are snow leopards and bears, but we never saw any.

The creature that has most caught the imagination is the yeti or Abominable Snowman, which according to folklore has been sighted on many occasions in the Tibetan–Himalayan area. While I was in Darjeeling, stories were circulating of how an army officer had encountered a very large ape-like creature while on a trek similar to ours. He was, however, a very heavy drinker and his story was understandably discounted. In 1951 Eric Shipton, the mountaineer, while crossing a high pass near Mount Everest, discovered and photographed a trail of huge footprints, possibly the tracks of an Abominable Snowman. As the creature was travelling in the same direction, Shipton's porters refused to go on. The problem was soon solved by Shipton's saying that, based on irrefutable evidence, the yeti was known to walk backwards! Local people we met certainly believed in the yeti and I too like to believe in its existence.

While we were climbing to cross over the Natu La and Jelep La passes (16,500 ft) and emerge onto the Tibetan Plateau, numerous Tibetan pony trains passed us on their way to Darjeeling to trade in yak wool. We could hear them approaching from a long way off by the tinkling of bells attached to the ponies. The women used to smell awful, rather like rancid cheese, and as they passed we laughed, held our noses with one hand and with the other made a movement like pulling a lavatory chain. Being the good-natured, pleasure-loving people they are, they replied with similar signs, obviously thinking that it was a form of religious greeting. One particular morning we heard a pony train coming towards us; as it passed I noticed to my amazement that there was a European amongst the Tibetans. To my further surprise he turned out to be Arthur Dee, who was a housemaster at Marlborough when I was still a pupil there. He was on a less ambitious trip than us and was on leave from a British artillery regiment. Ironically, he was an elderly captain while I was a schoolboy major, but the effect of the meeting was to take me immediately back to my schooldays!

The Tibetans were a most friendly people, and also extremely religious. When I visited the country it was ruled by the Dalai Lama, living in his palace at Lhasa. There were a large number of monasteries, where about a quarter of the male population lived and led a celibate life. The remainder of the population practised a mixture of monogamy, polygamy and polyandry!

On our return journey we stayed in a Buddhist monastery in Sikkim, at a place called Rinchenpong. This was a fascinating experience. The monks seemed to be obsessed by the fact that the pattern of life was like a circle and one should travel round this circle in a clockwise motion: for example, on entering a room the custom was always to go from right to left and never the reverse. Almost everything was considered to be either auspicious or inauspicious! Frequently on our trek we would encounter a small pile of stones called a *chorten*, and in order to propitiate Lord Buddha we would halt and, clasping our hands, walk around the *chorten* three times saying '*Om mane padme hum*'.* Occasionally we would come to a *mendong*, which had the same purpose as a *chorten*, but was a low wall and anything up to 100 yards in length. This could prove a major obstacle to our progress. Strange to say, I never felt like avoiding the ritual. Being in high mountains has a strange awe-inspiring effect, and it is easy to accept the necessity of placating the gods.

The crossing over the Natu La and Jelep La passes was arduous, for we so easily got out of breath. Once we had reached the snow line at an altitude of 13,000 feet, we had to wear snow shoes, which we had previously acquired. It was also particularly bleak, as we had left the tree line far behind us. One day, while staying by a frozen lake, we were visited by a group of Tibetan devil dancers, who put on a small display for us; I was lucky enough to get a photograph.

Some days later, when we were still short of Gyangze, my right thigh began to swell badly and caused considerable pain around my old wound. Walking became progressively more difficult and eventually we had to abandon the journey and return, with me riding one of our ponies. The mail was transferred to a group of traders going to Gyangze and we returned to Kalempong, a small tea-plantation town a few miles from Darjeeling, where I was admitted to a Mission hospital. From there I was transferred the following day in an ancient car to the Military Hospital in Darjeeling. We had been

* Meaning 'Hail to the jewel in the lotus'; associated with the Bodhisavattva of Compassion, Avalokiteswara, and thought to have a secret tantric meaning.

away nearly six weeks and must have trekked about 400 miles. It was now late May. The medical verdict was that I was suffering from thrombosis in the area of my wound and the best treatment was rest and hot poultices. I was confined to bed for about two weeks and it was not until the second week in July that I rejoined my Battalion in southern Burma at Pegu on the Sittang River.

This had been the most exciting and stimulating venture that I have ever undertaken. Although we never achieved our objectives, we did cross the Himalayas and travelled some way into Tibet. During the war years only a handful of people were able to make the same journey. It was only after the war was over that I was able to read Heinrich Harrer's wonderful book *Seven Years in Tibet*,* in which he describes how, as a German internee in India, he was able to escape and walk to Lhasa, where he became a tutor to the Dalai Lama. I learned far more from his book than I ever found out on my travels, but such is often the case. Today Tibet is no longer a mystical, unknown and 'forbidden country', but a militarized region of China known as Xizang Zizhighu. The Dalai Lama now lives in exile in India. The old magic has gone forever.


### The Forgotten War Ends, and it Rains Fishes

The Japanese were in almost total disarray at this time; they were fleeing south-westwards, without vehicles or air support, towards the sanctuary of Siam. They had fought hard and I felt pity for them. For the first time in the war I saw Japanese POWs; previously they had preferred suicide – by disembowelling themselves with a hand grenade – to captivity. Germany's surrender on 7 May had passed us by virtually unnoticed. Throughout 1945 the British press frequently referred to the war in Burma as 'The Forgotten War', and it was commonplace to refer to the forces in Burma as 'The Forgotten Army'.

While I was convalescing in India my Battalion carried out a successful ambush behind Japanese lines. The ambush, consisting of

* Heinrich Harrer, *Seven Years in Tibet*. Translated from the German by Richard Graves, with an introduction by Peter Fleming (London: R. Hart-Davis, 1953).

one officer and fifteen men, established itself under cover of darkness on a main road in Central Burma. Soon after they were in position two civilian cars came along with their headlights on. When the cars were abreast of the ambush, our soldiers opened fire on them, which resulted in chaos and shouting. The cars came to an abrupt halt, but the occupants somehow managed to get away, despite having been wounded. There was a fair amount of blood everywhere, including two bloodstained briefcases that belonged to an Indian brigadier of the 2nd Brigade of the Indian National Army. The Indian National Army (INA) was formed by the Japanese from Indian soldiers captured in Malaya and in Singapore. These Indian prisoners were separated from their British officers and became easy prey to propaganda aimed at inducing them to fight for the liberation of India. The majority, however, remained loyal.

When the war ended three leading officers of the INA stood trial by court martial for treason at the Red Fort in Delhi. The briefcases captured in the ambush provided part of the evidence against them. They were duly found guilty and sentenced to death, but were pardoned by the Viceroy, who was then Field Marshal Viscount Wavell.

When at Pegu we caught the final lashes of heavy rains and high winds of the monsoon. My orderly ran to tell me that it was raining fishes. There, outside my tent, was a pool of water with hundreds of silvery fish, 2–3 inches long, swimming happily about and looking as if they were having a rare old time. Our soldiers were in a great state of excitement and were trying to catch them by any means including cooking pots and their own clothing.

When I finally got back to England I found that my mother had a copy of a book called *Believe It or Not*,* written by an American called Robert Ripley. One of the amazing facts described in this book was how the strong winds in the monsoon could lift up into the sky masses of young spawning fish from the shallow shoals of the rivers; these fish were then delivered back to earth in the ensuing rain.

The Japanese 28th Army in Southern Burma were trying to escape eastwards across a large area known as the Pegu Yomas. The Yomas

* Robert L. Ripley, *Believe It or Not! A modern book of wonders, miracles, freaks, monstrosities and almost impossibilities* (New York: Simon and Schuster, 1929).

was not like the massive ranges of North Burma, thousands of feet high. Seen from the Mandalay–Rangoon road it comprised low-lying hills, which seemed to offer little difficulty in crossing, but their appearance is deceptive. They rise to about 1,800 ft and are approximately 80 miles long from north to south and 30 miles wide. They are thickly forested with bamboo and the hillsides are frequently precipitous. Much of the area is swamp, which in the monsoon turns into lakes and mud, and it was precisely at this period that the Japanese Army in retreat was passing through the Yomas. Additionally they had two further obstacles to pass: one was the Pegu–Rangoon road and the other was the Sittang River, now in full flood and three times its normal size. Troops withdrawing from south Arakan had also to cross the Irrawaddy River. Fortunately, the Japanese, better than most people, knew how to use bamboo. They could eat the young shoots, build shelters from the rain, and even make makeshift rafts. Their standard daily ration at this time was a gruel of rice and bamboo shoots supplemented with edible grasses, snails and lizards.

Fighting continued around 89 Brigade area at Pegu and eastwards towards the Sittang River, almost up to the time of the Japanese surrender. Off the roads movement was extremely difficult. The 4/8 Gurkhas were involved in a number of harassing actions and suffered moderate casualties floundering about in the waist-high water of the paddy fields. Being small of stature they suffered more than most, but the Japanese in general were small too, and suffered likewise.

We had captured detailed maps showing the Japanese escape routes, particularly the night crossing points over the Pegu road, which we then blocked with tanks and infantry, resulting in mass killings of fleeing Japanese, who never seemed to appreciate that their plans had been compromised and repeated the same mistakes night after night. We suffered very few casualties and it was impossible not to feel sympathy for those killed. They came on like relentless ants pursuing the same path. Many were sick, some were wounded and all were undernourished. Any decent soldier could not help thinking 'poor little buggers'.

A Japanese staff officer, Lieut. Col. Tanaka, wrote:

Before reaching the Sittang River I thought that I had already seen the extremes of suffering but it had been nothing to what

I saw on the approaches to the Sittang: soldiers with rotting feet, calves swollen to elephantine size with beri-beri, eyes burning with fever and many suffering from dysentery. The thought of approaching the Sittang River had of course spurred them on. The alternative was to die covered by flies with the vultures flying overhead.*

General Sukarai, the Commander of the 28th Army, made his way to the Sittang River and must have looked at the swirling torrent of water with mixed thoughts, for it was here that he had beaten the British three and a half years previously. All his achievements had now come to nothing. He recalls:

I crossed at 2 a.m. on 28 July in a local boat. When I looked back I could see that some of my men had not made it, and their tired bodies were whipped away downstream. I prayed that the Gods and Buddhas would protect us.*

Sakurai's horse had been drowned in the river, and he continued his journey on the back of an ox. Others who crossed at the same time as Sakurai were a party of comfort girls, who had cut their hair short in order to look like men.

Despite the fact that the Japanese had been well and truly beaten, the general feeling on our side was one of despondency in seeing no end to the war. We thought that there would be no general surrender, thus necessitating the recapture of Malaya and ultimately an invasion of Japan itself. The dropping of the two atomic bombs on Hiroshima and Nagasaki followed by the Japanese surrender on 14 August came as a complete surprise to us and was incomprehensible in its enormity.

The Japanese Emperor Hirohito made an announcement on the radio to his people in which he said that they would have to 'endure the unendurable'. For most individual Japanese surrender was simply unthinkable. How much more so at the national level? Somewhat later the Emperor denied his deity to an incredulous

* Allen, *Burma: The Longest War*.
* Ibid.

nation. It was very important to the Japanese military that after their surrender they would not be treated as prisoners of war. The Allies therefore decreed that they would be called 'Japanese surrendered personnel', or JSP; this was a euphemism, but it served a good purpose, for it allowed the Japanese to be responsible for their own administration and discipline.

Despite their formal surrender many Japanese, half-starved and ill-equipped, fought on, as they had lost touch with their own HQs and were unaware that the war was over. At this time my company was guarding an important railway bridge that crossed the Salween River. Daily I saw bloated corpses trapped in the back eddies of the river; they were covered in freshwater prawns, which were feeding off them. I vowed never to eat prawns again, but just as most resolutions in life get broken, it was only a few weeks later that I was eating delicious prawns in the restaurants of Siam.

It was almost impossible to grasp the fact that the war was now over. No longer would we be carrying our personal weapons wherever we went, nor sleeping with them ready to hand. No more 'standing to' at dawn and dusk. It would not be easy to put aside a whole way of life. What next, and where? We were soon to know, for our Division received orders to concentrate at Rangoon preparatory to flying into Siam in order to disarm the Japanese there and assist in the evacuation of our own POWs, who had been working on the notorious Burma–Siam railway.

Our motor convoys went past Lake Victoria on the outskirts of Rangoon, where my father had lived at the turn of the century when working for a large trading company. There are still some attractive-looking bungalows on the shores of the lake, and I wondered in which bungalow he had lived.

My lasting impressions of Rangoon were, first, the Shwe Dagon, a Buddhist Pagoda standing higher than St Paul's Cathedral, 368 feet high and coloured in real gold leaf; second, seeing attractive women, which made a welcome change from the cheroot-smoking old biddies in the villages through which we had advanced in the past months; and third, the awful squalor of the place after 3½ years of Japanese occupation.

On what was to be my last day in Rangoon I went to purchase some new clothes and underwear from a military shop set up by the Ordnance Corps. At the cash desk was a most beautiful girl. She was obviously Anglo-Burmese, for she spoke good English. She greeted me with a delightful smile; when I had paid my bill I unfortunately had to leave, as there was an impatient queue behind me. My father had once told me that Anglo-Burmese women were amongst the most beautiful and intelligent in the world and I got back to our tented camp firmly resolved to return to the shop the next day. However, I was greeted with the news that I was to command our advance party, which was to fly to Siam early the next morning. Our best-laid plans can so easily come to nought.

*Chapter 4*

# SIAM AND MALAYA

## Occupation of Siam

After we had been only two days in Rangoon sufficient aircraft had been assembled for the air movement into Siam to begin. In the early morning of 3 September we taxied down the runway of Mingaladon airfield, which was littered on either side with destroyed Japanese aircraft, to make the 400-mile flight to Bangkok.

I was in the first plane to land on the Bangkok airfield, which had been severely damaged by Allied bombing, but the Japanese had patched it up for our arrival. The control tower was manned by Japanese controllers. We circled the airfield once, then made our approach run, and after a bumpy landing taxied up to a badly damaged airport building, in front of which were paraded a large number of Japanese soldiers. I remember feeling somewhat scruffy, as I had been unable to complete my re-equipping purchases in Rangoon. I made sure that my fly-buttons were done up before I alighted from the aircraft in order that I would be worthy of being a member of a victorious Army. The sight of so many soldiers paraded closely together made me apprehensive as to what sort of reception we would receive. An English-speaking officer approached us and we explained that we were the first plane of the 'fly-in'. The personal behaviour, discipline and dignity of the Japanese were most impressive. Their faces were completely expressionless.

In the weeks ahead, as the process of disarming and concentrating some 115,000 Japanese troops continued, they earned the respect of everyone by their efficiency: orders given were always instantly obeyed. I was surprised to find no animosity towards the Japanese by our own soldiers, whether British or Indian, but then, of course, we had not been subjected to their cruelty as prisoners of war. My own experience has been that those most closely involved in fighting often have little hatred for their opponents.

The administrative problems were considerable, for besides having to disperse and accommodate the troops of our Division, we also had to arrange the fly-out of some 20,000 POWs, mostly British, who had been working on the infamous Burma Railway. To add to the pot-pourri there were also a number of Dutch and Indonesian ex-POWs who had to be repatriated.

During these early days in Siam I ordered a Japanese working party to find for us various items of sports gear, including footballs and hockey sticks. It was all part of a deliberate policy to keep our soldiers occupied physically and so reduce their ardour for the attractive Siamese women. The Japanese major showed neither surprise nor amusement. Two days later everything that I had asked for was delivered. I expect he thought that as a victorious Army we should be behaving differently and have our minds on other things.

Soon after we arrived I was sent west of Bangkok to the railhead of the Burma railway to help in the repatriation of British POWs. They were in good spirits and delighted to see their fellow-countrymen and to be on their way home. Not surprisingly, many were in poor physical shape and had to be carried on stretchers. Our aim was to fly them out of Siam as quickly as possible, on to Rangoon and to India. After a couple of weeks I rejoined the Battalion, which was quartered in the University of Bangkok. Our soldiers lived in well-ventilated classrooms and the Law Library became the Officers' Mess. Later I was sent to a charming seaside resort called Chonburi, some 60 miles from Bangkok on the Gulf of Siam. Our task was to ferry out armed guards to all merchant ships docking in Bangkok in order to safeguard their cargoes. When their tasks were completed they returned to Chonburi in requisitioned lorries.

I was lucky enough to have a small motor launch for my own personal use, manned by a couple of Siamese who were charming but incompetent. The weather was good and the setting was truly idyllic, complete with a lovely sandy beach offering excellent bathing. Seafood was plentiful and hardly a day went by without eating shrimps or prawns, usually deep fried with ginger and a touch of brown sugar. I had conveniently forgotten my vow never to eat prawns again. At night the view over the Gulf of Siam was fantastic, with the phosphorus glittering on the small breaking waves. My one fear was that our Utopian existence would be discovered and others would want to join us or, even worse, take it over from us. Late in October we received the bad news that we were to return to Bangkok and rejoin the rest of the Battalion in the University.

For the first time since leaving Kohima the Battalion was all together. We explored the city with its intricate network of canals, and tasted the various delicacies of the marvellous Chinese restaurants, which was a new experience for all of us. All the POWs had been repatriated long ago, and the Japanese military had also gone. We obtained some golf clubs and balls from somewhere and a few of us played on the Royal Thai Golf Course, which was good fun even though the course was in appalling condition. One afternoon, when we were about to drive off the first tee, a smiling Siamese golfer wearing a large straw hat, approached and said: 'Me number one golfer in Siam'. I made some fatuous reply, such as 'Jolly good show', whereupon he removed my tee and ball and substituted his own. He then did a perfect drive, raised his hat and walked off.

We spent a marvellous Christmas in Bangkok, but sadly our days in Siam were drawing to a close, for the 7th Indian Division had been warned to move to Malaya early in January. There were also rumours that because of the problems confronting the Dutch in re-occupying the Dutch East Indies we might be going to Java. The Indonesian war for independence from the Dutch had already begun and was to continue until 1949.

Our stay in Siam had been most enjoyable. The Siamese appeared for the most part to be charming, indolent and pleasure-seeking, with gambling as their favourite pastime; even two flies crawling up a wall would provide an excuse for a bet as to which fly would reach the top first. Other than my idyllic stay at Chonburi, my chief memories are of numerous Buddhist temples; attractive, gentle and graceful women; men carrying numerous glass bowls containing a single tiger fish, which, when placed with another tiger fish would fight to the death (a Siamese form of cock fighting); and those marvellous Chinese restaurants (the Chinese seemed to be the most resourceful part of the population).

At a dinner hosted by the Mayor of Bangkok there must have been at least thirty dishes, including 40-year-old eggs, which tasted like a cross between asparagus and mushrooms. Other interesting dishes

79

included small birds eaten whole, bones and all, stuffed dormice, and chrysanthemum and white fungus cakes. It was rumoured that a particular Chinese delicacy was to eat the uncooked brains of a freshly killed monkey; fortunately I never experienced this. Some years later when stationed in Hong Kong I heard the same story.

In late 1945 Supreme Allied Command South-East Asia decreed that all Japanese officers, other than those under arrest for war crimes, should formally surrender their swords. The main parade and ceremony in Bangkok took place in early January, when twenty-two generals and admirals surrendered their swords to General Evans, who had replaced Messervy as commander of the 7th Indian Division, and individually saluted and bowed before the Union Jack. Amongst those surrendering were the Commander of the 15th Army and five Divisional Commanders, including our old enemy General Hanaya from the Arakan.

All the various units of our Division were represented at the Parade and provided escorts for the wretched admirals and generals. The humiliation of the Japanese was complete and almost beyond belief. The 7/2nd Punjab Regiment was on the parade, but I unfortunately was away on detachment, and so missed seeing this most moving and unforgettable occasion. So ended our part in the war against Japan.

Towards the end of January we sailed for Singapore from Bangkok on the *Highland Brigade*, a sister ship of the *Highland Chieftain* on which I had set sail from the Clyde five years previously. Our Division was to become a part of the Malaysian land forces.

## A Close Shave in the Gulf of Siam

Two days before we were due to sail on the *Highland Brigade* I had further trouble with an old grenade wound in my right thigh, which had become badly swollen and made walking difficult, but as it was not considered to be serious I was allowed to embark. However, once aboard I found myself unable to walk at all, and furthermore felt feverish; I was consequently confined to my cabin. The 1,000-mile journey down the Gulf of Siam and then into the South China Sea was to take three days.

I cannot explain why I was not moved into the ship's sick bay;

perhaps the answer is that there was no such place. Surat Singh, my young Sikh orderly, looked after me as best as he could, and anyway I did not feel well enough to want much.

In the very early morning of the last day of our voyage (18 January) I was awakened by a large explosion followed by a great deal of commotion and alarm bells ringing. It turned out that we had hit a stray Japanese mine, some 60 miles from Singapore. The engine room had been holed and the engines put out of action. A radio message was passed to Singapore asking for assistance. The ship soon developed a very pronounced list, and all troops were ordered to their lifeboat stations. I lay in my cabin in complete darkness until Surat Singh, accompanied by two of our officers, led me with the aid of a torch up to the boat decks. It was eerie, moving through the darkened ship, which was so quiet that it seemed that everyone else had jumped overboard.

When I got to the boat deck dawn had already broken and there was a fair amount of daylight. I soon forgot my fears. The atmosphere was one of total calm, which in the dawn light, and not knowing the extent of our plight, was most impressive. I did reflect that it would be rough justice to be sunk by a stray mine five months after the war! Eventually, after about seven hours, two tugboats arrived to tow us into Singapore. Luckily the sea was calm and, with the aid of the tugs and the ship's pumps, we arrived safely. Our mishap had occurred only some 60 miles from where the battleships *Prince of Wales* and *Repulse* had been sunk by Japanese torpedo-carrying aircraft on 10 December 1941.

I left the *Highland Brigade* on a stretcher; this form of transport was by now almost becoming a way of life. The cause of my discomfort was quickly discovered to be a piece of jungle green cloth in my thigh, which had not previously shown up on the X-ray photos; it was removed under a general anaesthetic. A nursing sister kindly presented it to me in a little glass jar, but I had no wish to keep such a disgusting relic. In later life, at odd intervals, small fragments from the same Japanese hand grenade have made their presence known by popping out through my skin, particularly after a hot bath.

There did not seem to be any urgency to get back to my Battalion, which was now approximately 200 miles north of Singapore, near Kuala Lumpur. I had been advised to stay in hospital under observation for a few days, so I took this marvellous opportunity of having a good look at Singapore. In the five months or so since the war had ended a great deal had changed for the better, but Singapore had not yet recovered its pre-war glamour. Raffles Hotel was again in business and serving its world-renowned gin slings. Cricket too had restarted. For me, who had for so long been a sort of jungle bumpkin, it was sheer paradise; what is more, I had money to spend. At that time I had known of the existence of Changi Prison, but not of its terrible significance in having contained the greatest number of British and Australian POWs in the Far East. I very much regret that I did not visit it.

## Malaya

*Pre-war Malaya*
Pre-war Malaya comprised a number of separate parts. First, there were the Straits Settlements, of which Singapore Island was the most important; they were a Crown Colony ruled by a Governor. Then there were nine Federated Malay States, each ruled by a Sultan but under British protection; and finally there were four unfederated States, which had been ceded to Britain by Siam in 1909. Malaya became an independent country in 1957 and Singapore, with its largely Chinese population, ultimately became an independent republic in 1965.

After leaving hospital in Singapore I rejoined my Battalion in Seremban in Negri Sembilan, 120 miles to the north. Shortly after my arrival we moved again further north to Taiping, which was only some 50 miles from the Siamese border.

Our Divisional HQ was in Taiping. One morning I received a message from the Adjutant that I was to report urgently to General Evans. This worried me; I could not think of any possible reason why he would want to see me. I duly reported and the General told me that I was to write the Divisional history of the Seventh Indian Division from the time of its formation in India to the end of the Burma campaign. I protested that I was no writer; that I had had only a microscopic view of operations; and, furthermore, that those closest to events were usually least qualified to write about them. He replied that I was about the only infantry major who had survived the whole period of operations (despite having been wounded three times) and was now available in Malaya. I thought this was a silly argument, but the General was adamant.

I was given a small bungalow in which to work, plus a very pleasant Anglo-Chinese lady shorthand typist. She, with a university degree, was somewhat better educated than me, for although I had passed the Oxford and Cambridge University entrance examination the onset of war had prevented me from actually going up to university. For nearly three months I worked in Divisional HQ and, armed with the General's authority, had access to all relevant documents including, of course, the war diaries of all units. My initial reaction was to feel that I had been given a 'kick up the backside', for I worked long hours and had great difficulty in assembling and annotating information. My brother officers in the Battalion seemed to be having one hell of a good time. Much later I was appreciative of the opportunity I had been given, to work on something in which I had no experience. What I produced was, after further editing, published as the official history of the Golden Arrow Division.*

Later I became friendly with the Chief Colonial Police Officer in the area and we used to shoot wild boar together. One day he asked me whether I would like to visit the local prison and see some senior Japanese officers who had been tried for war crimes and were condemned to death by hanging. I said that I would like to see them, but I was appalled to find them looking like caged beasts, in cells fronted with iron bars. With their cropped hair and prison clothes they were a pathetic sight. They had, however, still retained their dignity and somehow made me feel small in comparison with them. I was horrified when it was suggested that I might like to be an official witness at their execution. I heatedly explained that I had no animosity whatsoever towards them and would find the whole thing nauseating.

## The Dickie Jones Affair

After the fall of Singapore a guerrilla movement trained by the British (Force 136) and consisting mainly of Chinese Communists operated within Malaya against the Japanese; they called themselves

* The Golden Arrow was our Divisional emblem.

the Malay People's Anti-Japanese Army (MPAJA). In 1945 this Force numbered nearly 7,000. After the Japanese surrender the vast majority handed in their arms, but a hard core of Communists remained in the jungles with the aim of making Malaya a Communist state. In 1946 the occasional Communist ambushes occurred on the jungle roads.

Taiping lies in an old tin-mining area and was the centre of serious inter-faction fighting in the mid-nineteenth century. Rival Chinese dialect groups and secret societies fought to gain dominance in the area; so disruptive and dangerous was the fighting that the British colonial authorities marked the eventual end of conflict by naming the settlement *Taiping* – the Chinese word for 'great peace'. This is an interesting historical point, because this area around Taiping had always been subject to disorder and anti-government terrorist activities. In 1945 it still retained that reputation, especially around Grik, right up in the mountains near the Siam border.

From Taiping the land rises in steep, jungle-covered ridges northwards towards Siam. The views from these mountains are magnificent, or at least they are when the rain and mists clear, for this area has perhaps the highest rainfall in Malaya, at over 200 inches a year. Here in the darkness of the lawless jungle fringes among the headwaters of the Perak River the country is ideal for terrorist activity, particularly as the few inhabitants are either scattered Malay farmers or simple nomadic aboriginal people known locally as the Semang. The rainforest has in a few places been taken over by rubber plantations, the trees planted in straight lines and their branches meeting overhead to produce a wonderfully dappled light in what look like great cathedral naves.

Soon after arriving in Taiping I went with the Brigade Intelligence Officer, whom I shall call Dickie Jones (not his real name), to investigate a shooting incident at Grik near the Siamese border. We were totally unaware of the bad reputation of the area and set off in a light-hearted mood, armed only with pistols, to enjoy a day away from Taiping. We travelled by jeep, driven by a Sikh driver from my Battalion, and also accompanied by one armed escort. As we ascended the road towards Grik we remarked on how forbidding the countryside looked, particularly the sunless rubber plantations. During our journey we met no one on the road, nor did we see any signs of life anywhere. Our original carefree attitude slowly evapo-

1. British and Viceroy Commissioned Officers of the 7/2nd Punjab Regiment in Madras, 1942. The author is standing in the second row, third from left.

2. A picture given to me by my Subedar Allah Dad, my Company second-in-command.
I was moved by his gift for he presented it to me as a sort of talisman before we
entered the Arakan. It shows, I think, Mohammed with some of his disciples. As I
treasured it, I had it sent back to our Depot for safe-keeping.

Allah Dad was a fine man. He was, of course, much older than me, probably in his
late thirties and was, in a sense, a father figure. He combined his loyalty to me with
courtesy and a wry sense of humour. He had the respect of every single soldier in his
Company. He was killed towards the end of the Japanese Arakan offensive.

3. The Battalion included three different classes of soldiers. Left, a Sikh, below a Punjabi Mussulman and a Dogra.

4. Mules carrying water and ammunition to a forward infantry company. Due to the almost complete absence of roads, each forward unit had a quota of mules, most of which were imported from the Middle East. *(Imperial War Museum)*.

5. A Japanese photo showing the first train to run on the infamous Siam/Burma railway. The ill-treatment of our prisoners-of-war who were forced to help construct the railway under appalling conditions, resulting in a heavy loss of life, has been the cause of lasting bitterness.

6. Indian infantry preparing to attack a Japanese position in the Arakan. *(Imperial War Museum).*

7. A jeep convoy rounding one of the many bends on the deeply-rutted Jessami track, running east from Kohima. *(Imperial War Museum).*

8. Close to my Company position looking south along the Kohima Ridge towards the ruins of the District Commissioner's bungalow and Naga Village. In the far distance buildings of Kohima Town can be seen. *(Imperial War Museum)*.

9. A scene of devastation on one of the numerous Japanese positions on the Kohima Ridge. *(Imperial War Museum)*.

10. A Gurkha soldier inspecting what was once a Japanese bunker.
*(Imperial War Museum).*

11. Gurkha soldiers clearing a Japanese bunker by using phosphorous grenades.
A dead Japanese lies in front. *(Imperial War Museum)*.

12. After the battles some of our Sikh Company relaxing with Battalion 2 I/C,
    Rupert Rowland.

13. Admiral Lord Louis Mountbatten, Supreme Commander South East Asia,
    presenting gallantry awards at Kohima. Colonel Mainprise King (Dahti Fahti),
    my Commanding Officer, is standing to the left of Admiral Mountbatten.

14. Four generals driving in a jeep after the capture of Mandalay. In front from left to right: General Bill Slim (14th Army Commander), Major General Pete Reese (19 Indian Division). In rear General Montague Stopford (Commander 33 Corps) and ? *(Imperial War Museum)*.

15. At the conclusion of the war General Itagaki (Japanese Army Commander) surrendered his sword to General Messervy, then GOC Malaya Command, who received it on behalf of the Supreme Allied Commander. The photograph was taken at H.Q. Malaya Command, Kuala Lumpur. *(Imperial War Museum)*.

16. Soldiers wearing life jackets at a lifeboat station after the *Highland Brigade* had hit a mine.

17. Hong Kong before its rapid postwar development. This photograph was taken in 1950 from the Peak looking across the harbour to the Kowloon peninsula. In the background are the New Territories. The naval base is in the right foreground.

18. Arrival of the Middlesex at Pusan aboard HMS *Unicorn* (aircraft carrier). They received a warm welcome from the Koreans, including the Korean "beauty" in the photograph.

19. US "veterans" of the Korean War welcome the first British troops to arrive. In the centre is Captain John Slim of the Argyll and Sutherland Highlanders, son of Field Marshal Viscount Slim; the author, then a captain in the Middlesex Regiment, is on the left.

20. Bringing in a Chinese Prisoner of War

21. South Korean refugee, carrying her injured child, passes a dead Korean in the foreground. The vast number of Korean refugees was a tragic feature of the war. *(Imperial War Museum)*.

22. The Middlesex spearheading the advance with US Patton tanks south of the Manchurian border.

23. Patrol in the bleak snow-covered hills of North Korea.

24. A typical battle-scarred Korean village.

25. The author as a Lieutenant-
Colonel in 1968.

26. The author with Japanese war hero Major Nishida wearing kimonos after nude bathing in hot-water springs at Hakone.

27. The author with Japanese veteran Mr Hirakubo standing near the epicentre of the atomic bomb on Hiroshima. The domed constuction is the only surviving building.

rated and we reached Grik slightly apprehensive as to what we would find.

We parked our jeep in a rubber plantation, telling our driver and escort to remain with the vehicle while we, armed only with our pistols, made our way across a small clearing to some *atap* (palm-thatched) huts on a small hillock. I led the way and concentrated on looking at the *atap* huts ahead. Suddenly I was brought to a standstill by stumbling against the body of a Chinese lying on his back. He had blood on his face and I presumed that he had been shot. As I turned to warn Dickie, we were fired on by a light machine-gun from about 200 yards away. I told Dickie to run like hell and rendezvous at our vehicle. I remember jumping over an irrigation ditch, and on reaching our jeep expected Dickie to arrive almost immediately. I waited for nearly three hours but then, as it was getting dark, we made our way back to Taiping and I rather shamefacedly had to report that Dickie was missing.

A week later we got a written message from Dickie, delivered by a Chinese coolie, saying that he had been captured by Communist guerrillas and requesting a toothbrush, toothpaste and cigarettes. These were duly dispatched through Chinese intermediaries. A further three weeks passed and eventually a total of some 3,000 troops were deployed searching the jungles, but with no results. I was now merely a passive spectator to events.

Colonel Spencer Chapman,* the leader of Force 136, who had spent three years operating in the jungles behind Japanese lines and in 1945 got away by submarine only to return by parachute before the Japanese surrender, managed to arrange Dickie's release by paying a ransom of 50,000 US dollars. I never saw Dickie again. His story was that when running away he fell in a ditch and hid, hoping that he would not be found, which sadly was not the case. He said that at one stage he had been tied to a tree and threatened that his liver would be fried in front of him if he attempted to escape. He wanted to sell this unlikely story to the Press, but was forbidden to do so and he was sent back to England.

This event was in fact a prelude to the Malayan Emergency, which involved British and Commonwealth forces suppressing these

---

* His best-known book is *The Jungle is Neutral* (London: Chatto & Windus, 1949).

selfsame Chinese Communist guerrillas throughout a period of eight years (1948–56)

The Emergency began officially in June 1948. It followed the shift in tactics by the Malayan Communist Party from its so-called 'moderate' line of agitation, through penetration of labour and other organizations, to outright guerrilla warfare, operating from within the protective cover of the Malayan jungle. Much of the rural population was scattered beyond the bounds of effective administration and often completely at the mercy of the terrorists. In order to combat the activities of the terrorists the authorities resettled populations in 'New Villages'. Some of the Chinese resettled in these villages were agriculturalists, who had settled before the war, but in the main they were townspeople, tin mine workers or rubber tappers who had gone into the countryside voluntarily or otherwise during the Japanese occupation. Many were driven there by food shortages and very few had obtained title to the land on which they were settled. Living in isolated communities, these squatters were exposed to terrorist intimidation and extortion, and became an important source of supplies, information and recruitment to the terrorists.

While this policy of resettlement worked quite well, it was not enough to bring the Emergency to a speedy conclusion. Malaya was to be plagued by armed internal insurrection, especially in the Grik area, which was to be the last area in the peninsula to be controlled by Communist forces. With hindsight it is now quite easy to see that Dickie Jones and I in early 1946 quite unwittingly had approached a key centre of the Malayan Chinese Communist movement and were lucky to escape with our lives. I have often wondered who the dead Chinese was and why he was killed. The short answer is that I will never know. My guess is that he was one of the guerrillas who had been executed for being a traitor.

Dickie Jones was certainly the only British officer ever to be captured by the Chinese Communists. There could so easily have been two.


## Last Days in the Indian Army

In June the Battalion moved to Kuala Lumpur, where we had an interesting little culinary problem: we were issued with a ration of

86

dehydrated whale meat in large oblong tins. No Indian soldier had ever seen a whale and it was difficult to explain that it was an aquatic mammal that sometimes reached 50 feet in length. As Muslims insist on eating only meat from which the source has had its throat cut (*halal*), and the Hindus insist that it had been killed by having its head cut off (*jatkar*), we had problems. Furthermore the meat looked like raw steak.

At this time I was Second-in-Command of my Battalion and the CO asked me to hold a meeting with all our senior Indian officers to gauge their feelings.

He said, 'Shippy, we have never ever lied to our soldiers and we are not going to start now. Remember also that the whale is not a fish, and you cannot appease Muslims by saying that it has had its throat cut, nor Hindus by saying that it has had its head cut off.'

I quickly realized that issuing whale meat to Indian troops was a non-starter; I advised the CO accordingly and called off the meeting. In the end the rations were withdrawn for Indian troops, so possibly avoiding a repetition of the disastrous Indian Mutiny of 1857, when Muslim troops were issued with bullets that had been treated with pig fat, which is obnoxious to their faith.

Days were now fast running out for me and in the second week of July I went to Singapore to board the Cunard liner *Mauretania* to return to England. To say that I was sad at leaving would be an enormous understatement, for I had very deep feelings of affection for all our Indian soldiers – Muslim, Sikh and Dogra. They had served the Raj with unstinting loyalty and were prepared, when called upon, to die for their Regiment (I say 'Regiment' quite deliberately, for that is where their focus of loyalty lay). Surat Singh, my young Sikh orderly, accompanied me and my baggage to the docks. He bade me farewell, saluted and said the Sikh battle cry '*Sul Sri Akal*' (God is strong), which I had heard so often. I didn't dare look back.

## Going Home

I boarded the SS *Mauretania* along with some 2,400 other service-men, some of whom had not seen England for over seven years. I had hoped to find a few old friends on board, but it was not to be.

The only person that I knew was the senior police officer in Taiping, Dicky Coombe, who was returning to England with his attractive wife. I imagine that they both must have been prisoners of the Japanese, but they never spoke about it.

Our ship was the successor to the original *Mauretania*, built in 1907. She was very modern (35,700 tons), and had been launched just before the outbreak of the war. At that time she was the largest ship to have sailed through the Suez Canal. She had been designed for comfort, but with her present complement conditions were very cramped, and despite my skills acquired in jungle navigation I spent a considerable amount of my time in getting lost. Early on in the voyage I was introduced to the drink Black Velvet, made with Guinness and champagne. Drunk from a tankard it is a splendid drink and a marvellous pick-me-up. We drank a lot of it. 'Greenhorn' that I was, having missed my youth in England, I had never drunk the stuff before.

Our voyage was uneventful, stopping only at Colombo, Aden and Port Said. The most memorable events for me were arriving at Aden and seeing the Union Jack proudly flying from Government buildings, and experiencing a somewhat stupid feeling that we were almost home and sailing through the Suez Canal. (Aden later became the decrepit and impoverished capital of the South Yemen Democratic Republic.) After Aden we passed through the Red Sea, the Gulf of Suez, the Bitter Lakes and the Suez Canal. The Canal was particularly impressive, lined by a seemingly endless succession of military camps with their stores, depots, vehicles of all kinds, and football pitches marked out in the desert sand. Everywhere there were distinctive regimental and corps flags flying in the slight breeze. At times we passed so close to the shore that those aboard could easily shout to those ashore and exchange the usual good-humoured and ribald greetings that soldiers indulge in. We unconsciously adopted the role of 'veterans' returning from the wars, for those ashore looked mere youngsters, with their white knees and faces.

There were few recreational amenities on the ship, for all available space was taken up by accommodation. There was therefore plenty of time to sit back and think. My thoughts were understandably mixed. I was sad to be leaving the Indian Army, probably never to return to India. I was glad to be going to see my mother, but apprehensive about returning to England, which I knew was going to be very different after so many years of war. My strong card was that I knew what I was going to do, for it was after the Battle of Kohima that I had put in an application to attend an Officers' Selection Board with the aim of obtaining a Regular Commission. Fortunately I passed the Selection Board in Calcutta and was later granted a Regular Commission in the Middlesex Regiment. My aim was to make the Army my career. Unlike so many of my compatriots I knew where I was heading.

Our port of disembarkation was the then great port of Liverpool. As we approached the Mersey there was a tremendous air of excitement. It was evening when we finally came alongside Prince's Landing Stage and in typical Liverpudlian style it was raining. Emergency arrangements had been made for making telephone calls; as far as I remember a three-minute call was free, which was fortunate for none of us had any English money. I was able to speak to my mother, which was a great thrill, as I had not heard her voice for well over five and a half years.

The following day we dispersed by train to various transit camps, where we spent some 24 hours being indoctrinated in how to live in post-war Britain, rather as if we were arriving in a foreign land. We all had a medical inspection to ensure that none of us was suffering from any dreadful eastern disease; we were then issued with ration books for clothing and food. We were also provided with money and the necessary arrangements were made for us to receive our pay and allowances. Additionally, we were all given a ready-made suit of a rather hideous pattern. I later gave my suit to a grateful gardener who worked in the gardens opposite my mother's flat in London. Finally, we received railway warrants to take us home and we were given some four weeks' leave.

We were all totally unprepared for the austerity of post-war Britain, with its stringent rationing (one egg per week and only a morsel of meat; car owners got sufficient petrol for only 300 miles per month). For the first time it began to dawn on me that I was totally ill-equipped for what might be termed 'normal living'. I had no suit, other than that given to me in Liverpool, or any warm clothing of any sort, for my heavy baggage was being forwarded from the Depot at Meerut and might take up to three months to arrive. In the meantime I had only a few civilian oddments, plus my jungle green uniforms, two Gurkha *kukris* and a mosquito net: all most useful in a wet and cold England. When my trunk finally did arrive the contents were useless, for they had been unused for five years and were unfit even for a jumble sale.

At last I was home. I was absolutely thrilled to see my mother again, who despite her worries throughout the war, none of which she ever mentioned, looked well and was full of good humour. She was living in a comfortable flat at Warwick Square, SW1. I certainly found it difficult to readjust; in particular confined spaces upset me and for some time I felt nervous when in a darkened cinema or theatre.

There is no better way to end what I have written on the Burma War than General Frank Messervy's Special Order of the Day, promulgated before the Division finally broke up, Indian units to return to India and British units to return to the United Kingdom. Below is a slightly abridged version:

### Special Order of the Day
### by
### Lieutenant-General Sir Frank Messervy, KBE, CB, DSO
### GOC-in-C, Malaya Command

*To all ranks of the 7th Indian Division*

It is now just over three years since the 7th Indian Division left RANCHI to fight the Japanese in BURMA. During that time it has been my proud privilege to command the Division during its first sixteen months in action, later to have it under my command in IV Corps in BURMA and finally in MALAYA Command.

I will recall the main actions which have made the Golden Arrow an emblem to be worn with pride by those entitled to it.

The fighting in the ARAKAN valley in February and March 1944 resulted in the major defeat inflicted on the Japanese by British forces. It was on the 7th Division that the brunt of that fighting fell. All units of the Division won glory in that fierce fight; all ranks came to know their superiority over the savage foe who up to then many had thought to be almost invincible.

Then came the tough battle of KOHIMA in rain and mud in

May and June, 1944. A stern battle in which the enemy had all the advantages of a position dug deep on the tops of a commanding ridge. The heights were finally won. The enemy's offensive on India was shattered. Pursuing them by tracks and paths through the vast mountains of the NAGA Hills, overcoming immense physical difficulties in the height of the monsoon, UKHRUL was captured.

The Division was next, after a well-earned rest, destined to lead the advance of IV Corps up to the IRRAWADDY River in early 1945. It was part of General SLIM'S bold and decisive outflanking drive to place IV Corps at MEIKTILA 100 miles behind the enemy's forward lines.

The Division eventually debouched exactly on time on the more open plain of the IRRAWADDY. Before the enemy could grasp what was happening, the mighty river, 1,000 yards of water at its narrowest point, was crossed on St Valentine's Day, 14 February 1945, near PAGAN, the ancient Capital of BURMA. The bridgehead for the advance of IV Corps on MEIKTILA was secured and firmly held.

The Division advanced on the YENANGYAUNG oilfields and captured them, subsequently moving south along the river axis and taking its toll of the enemy in several sharp engagements. Finally RANGOON was won.

But the war was not yet over and the Division fought its last battle, again in the SITTANG River area east of PEGU. Here, in dreadful conditions of heaviest monsoon downpour men moving waist-deep in waterlogged swamps and rice-fields, the Division drove back the enemy's final counter-attack in July 1945.

The war was over but we still had work to do. Moving by air and sea BANGKOK was occupied, the Japanese surrender taken and SIAM freed.

The final task of the Division has been an occupational one in NORTH MALAYA, where it has done good work to help in the rehabilitation of the country.

Now the Division is to return to INDIA. To all ranks of all units of the Division I can truly say that you can look back on your past with the greatest pride in your achievements and full satisfaction in a job well done. Your success has been won by courage, by efficiency and by tireless endeavour. Above all the Divisional spirit which has infused all ranks has inspired you and led you to final Victory. It has won for many of you honours and awards for gallantry and devotion to duty, including no less than four Victoria Crosses.

I thank you all from my heart for the many and glorious deeds you have done when serving under me. I wish you all the best of luck.

F.W. MESSERVY
Lieutenant-General GOC-in-C
Malaya Command.

The 7th Battalion returned to Jubbulpore in India in November 1946. In view of its distinguished war record, the Commander-in-Chief, Sir Claude Auchinleck, held a special investiture parade at which he presented honours and awards. The Battalion was later disbanded. In 1947 India and Pakistan became independent countries.

Of those who are still alive the Punjabi Mussulmans are no doubt all in Pakistan and only the Sikhs and Dogras remain in India. It is sad that men who fought side by side in close comradeship now find themselves divided by a newly created frontier, and to add insult to injury their respective countries have been at war with each other, both in East Pakistan (now Bangladesh) and also along the Kashmir border.

In 1983 my wife and I made a long visit to India, for I wanted to see what a modern, independent and democratic India looked like. When we were in Delhi we received a quite unexpected invitation to a drinks party, which had been arranged in order that I could meet old Regimental friends. General Jagit Singh Aurora, a former Colonel of the Regiment, who won fame as the victorious commander of the Indian Army in Bangladesh, was present. But the greatest surprise of all was to meet two Sikhs who had served with me and had been wounded in the Arakan battles. It was wonderful to see them again.

The 2nd Punjab Regiment no longer exists as such, but the Regimental badge has been adopted by the Punjab Regiment that I saw, when in Delhi, taking part in the Republic Day Parade. It was a thrill to see their immaculate turn-out and precision. After the

Parade I was invited by the then Colonel of the Punjab Regiment to attend a 'tea party' for all those who took part. He asked me to talk to the soldiers, in Urdu, of course, which for me was a special honour. To my eyes they looked exactly the same as those keen-eyed, sharp and fun-loving young men who had served in my Regiment some 40 years previously.

In 1988, while our son Michael was in Delhi as a First Secretary at the British High Commission, my wife and I visited India again. Michael arranged to accompany me to visit the Punjab Regiment Training Centre near Ranchi in Bihar, not far from where we did our training before going to the Arakan in 1943. We were treated with the customary military kindness and hospitality, and were guests of honour at a dinner in the Officers' Mess at which the Regimental Band played many of the old wartime favourites such as 'Doing the Lambeth Walk' and 'Colonel Bogey'. The whole evening was enhanced by the officers' wives attending the dinner in their beautiful and varied coloured saris. Afterwards Colonel Ahluwallah, the Centre Commander, made a charming speech of welcome, to which I replied. Having been in wartime India I had never before dined where the Regimental Colours and silver were displayed.

The following day I was invited by Colonel Ahluwallah to attend a *durbar* (an audience levee) at 7 a.m. at which all ranks, numbering about 1,200, were to be present, seated in a semicircular amphi-theatre. He had warned me only the night before at the dinner that he would like me to speak in Hindustani, using a microphone; this filled me with understandable apprehension. I spoke somewhat inadequately about my warmth of feeling for the past and wished them all success for the future. What I said appeared to be well received.

Later we were shown the Regimental Museum, where there were exhibits of Japanese weapons that the 7/2nd Battalion had captured in Burma. It was a moving experience to see the names of all those who had been recipients of awards for gallantry displayed on boards – British and Indian; officers and men. The one common denomi-nator was that they all had been 'comrades in arms'. I left Ranchi to return to Delhi deeply moved.

*Chapter 5*

# NOTES ON THE BURMA CAMPAIGN

## Organization of the 7/2 Punjab Regiment

Our composition was common to most Punjab Battalions: that is, roughly 50 per cent Mussulman, 25 per cent Sikh and 25 per cent Dogra. We never had any problems over class: Mussulmans, Hindus and Sikhs worked in complete harmony throughout the war and up to the time of the partition of India.

There were also a number of one-class regiments in the Indian Army, such as the Gurkhas and the Sikhs.

*Ranks*
The King's Commissioned Officers (that is, British or Indian with a commission from the Sovereign) in the battalion numbered at the most only fifteen. As the war progressed there was an increasing number of Indian officers, who served with great distinction. All the Viceroy Commissioned Officers (VCOs) were Indian, and their nearest equivalent ranks in the British Army, along with the NCOs, are shown below:

| *Indian* | *British* |
| --- | --- |
| Subedar Major* (VCO) | No British equivalent |
| Subedar (VCO) | Company 2 I/C |
| Jemedar (VCO) | Platoon Commander |
| Havildar Major | Company Quartermaster Sergeant |

* The Subedar Major was in fact a far more important rank than a RSM: he was the adviser to the Commanding Officer on all major issues affecting the Indian ranks.

94

| Indian | British |
|---|---|
| Havildar | Sergeant |
| Naik | Corporal |
| Lance Naik | Lance Corporal |
| Sepoy | Private Soldier |

*Battalion strength*
The theoretical strength of a battalion can be taken as being around 750 all ranks. In my experience the actual strength at any one time fluctuated between 550 and 700, and could at crisis periods fall even lower.

*Outline organization*
At **Battalion HQ** there was the Commanding Officer (a Lieutenant Colonel), the Second-in-Command (a Major), the Adjutant (a Captain) and the Intelligence Officer (a Captain or a Lieutenant)

The **Headquarters Company** comprised Quartermaster, Signals, Transport (mechanical or mules or both), and a 3-inch mortar platoon (six mortars with a range of approximately 3000 yards, firing high-explosive or smoke bombs).

The **rifle companies** were what might be termed the 'cutting edge' of the Battalion. We had four:

A    Punjabi Mussulman
B    Punjabi Mussulman
C    Sikh
D    Dogra

In each company there were three platoons, commanded by a Jemedar, and in each platoon there were three sections, commanded by a Naik. The theoretical strength of a platoon was thirty and that of a section eight.

What **transport** a battalion used depended entirely on the terrain. In the Arakan our mobility came from our feet. We also had a few four-wheel-drive jeeps, plus trailers and a number of mules. Much later during the advance into Central Burma we were initially moved south in 3-ton trucks, but the major part of our journey, the last 200 miles to the Irrawaddy River, was covered on our feet with the assistance of mules, mostly from a specialized Mule Company. Indian soldiers easily adapted to becoming muleteers and took a pride in their animals.

For **communications**, in static positions we used the field telephone, with a central exchange at Battalion Headquarters. This was most unsatisfactory, as the lines continually got cut for numerous different reasons (artillery and mortar fire, mules, human activity and sometimes wild animals). At platoon and company level we had radio communications but they were generally unsatisfactory, mainly because of interference by the terrain.

**Messing** was no problem: each company had its own very basic cooking facilities and provided its own cooks. When platoons were of mixed class composition, individual prejudices were 'swept under the carpet'. The basic diet was chapattis or rice and dhal (a form of pulse) plus a liberal ration of tinned milk, tea and sugar.

When static and not on operations we always established an officers' mess using British rations supplemented by local purchase (if available).

For **medical** support we usually had an Indian doctor (Indian Army Medical Corps) with us, who with a minimal staff would establish a Regimental Aid Post (RAP). Medical evacuation was by stretcher and jeep to a forward airfield. There were, of course, no helicopters. Evacuation was always a major problem.


## Personal equipment

I carried with me:

- Thompson sub-machine gun with at least five filled magazines, or Sten gun
- Hand grenade (primed)

- Very pistol for signalling with coloured flares
- First aid field dressing
- Water bottle plus purification tablets
- Sulphonamide powder for infected foot-ulcer sores
- Torch
- Basic washing kit
- Map case
- Towel
- Binoculars
- Change of underwear and socks
- Magnetic compass
- Ground sheet.

My large pack weighed about 45 pounds.

## Language

The language common to all ranks was Urdu, a form of Hindustani. Today Urdu is the language of Pakistan. Except in the Officers' Mess, English was not spoken. Our soldiers interspersed their Urdu with a fair sprinkling of Punjabi words and expressions, which soon became familiar. None of our soldiers, including the Subedars and Jemedars, spoke any English.

## The Order of Battle of the 7th Indian Division

The details given below cover the period from Ranchi in August 1943 until the Japanese surrender in August 1945.

Commanders:   Major General F.W. Messervy CB DSO
(Later Lieut. General Sir Frank Messervy, KBE, CB, DSO)
Major General G.C. Evans CBE, DSO
(Later Lieut. General Sir Geoffrey Evans, KBE, CB, DSO)

*Cavalry*

When we entered the Arakan the Division included the 3rd Gwalior Lancers, which had been provided by the Maharajah of Gwalior from his own State Forces. Two Squadrons were mounted not on chargers but on ponies, and carried out reconnaissance duties. They added a certain element of colour to the Burmese scene, but sadly they were not successful.

Two regiments of tanks from the Royal Armoured Corps supported the Division at different times: 25th Dragoons in the Arakan, and 116 Regiment (Gordons) in the final battle in South Burma.

*Artillery*
- 136 Field Regiment
- 139 Field Regiment
- 25 Mountain Regiment

(*Note*: The Field Regiments fired 25-pound shells. The Mountain Regiment had a smaller gun and was transported by mules.)

- 24 Anti Aircraft and Anti Tank Regiment

(*Note*: They had little opportunity to carry out their primary roles but they were closely involved as infantry in the Arakan.)

*Engineers*

There were three Field Companies (Indian Engineers). They were probably the hardest-worked troops in the Division, nearly always occupied in road and bridge construction, using bulldozers, local labour and elephants.

*Infantry*

114 Indian Brigade:
- Somerset Light Infantry
- 21 South Lancashire (April 1944 – June 1945)
- 4/14 Punjab Regiment
- 4/5 Royal Gurkha Rifles

33 Indian Brigade:
- 1 Queen's Royal Regiment (West Surrey)

- 4/15 Punjab Regiment
- 4/1 Gurkha Rifles
- 1 Burma (June 1944 – April 1945)

89 Indian Brigade:
- 2 King's Own Scottish Borderers
- 7/2 Punjab Regiment (August 1944 – August 1945 Divisional Recce Regiment)
- 1/11 Sikh
- 4/8 Gurkha Rifles

*Services*
- **Transportation:** The Royal Indian Army Service Corps (RIASC), comprising both motor transport and mule companies.
- **Medical:** Three Indian field ambulance units.
- **Workshops:** Three workshop companies for vehicle repairs.
- **Police:** Military police unit.
- **Intelligence:** Intelligence unit, which included Japanese-speaking interpreters.
- **Veterinary:** Small unit for care of mules.

The above details amply illustrate the complexity and diversity of a Division in the difficult terrain of Burma. We who served in what might be termed the fighting units were largely ignorant of what went on to the rear of us.


## The Officers

Except in one or two instances I have deliberately avoided identifying individuals; if I had done so the reader would have become bemused by a miscellany of names. Relative to our average overall strength of only fourteen officers, the number of casualties was high, as was wastage due to sickness.

Throughout the war the commanding officer and the second-in-command were regulars, and in the early years at least one company commander was usually a regular. These officers had been trained at Sandhurst in England and had then done a year's attachment with a British battalion in India before joining their Indian regiment. The pre-war officers were all volunteers and had been attracted to India by a more exciting style of life, which they could enjoy on higher rates of pay. Before the war it was often necessary to have a private income to join the more elite British regiments. To be selected for the Indian Army one had to have passed out of Sandhurst reasonably high in the order of merit. I met many regular Indian Army officers during the war and they were all, without exception, men of the highest integrity and for whom I had respect. Furthermore they had a love for and interest in their soldiers.

In the early years of the war a decision was made to increase considerably the size of the Indian Army and drafts of suitably qualified young men were sent out from England for training in India to receive 'Emergency Commissions' (ECOs). I was one. The understanding was that if an officer cadet failed to qualify as an officer he would remain in India and be posted to a British unit in the rank of private soldier.

Our defeats in Burma in 1942 and early 1943 were considered by some to be in part the result of too rapid an expansion of the Indian Army. This may well be true, but British units fared equally badly. My own opinion on looking back after a lifetime of soldiering was that our preparedness for Burma was initially poor. We also had little or no knowledge of the Japanese soldier and his training. Perhaps this is not surprising as our early training was most unimaginative. In the event ECOs fought in Burma with great distinction, helped by the fact that they were all volunteers for the Indian Army and had wonderful soldiers to lead.

In the six months covering operations in the Arakan, September 1943 – February 1944, we had three commanding officers. The first was evacuated suffering from a nervous breakdown after only six weeks. The second, Robin Rouse, was killed leading an attack in what was to be our last battle in The Arakan. He was brave, unconventional and much loved by our soldiers. The third, who took us to Kohima and Central Burma, was Terence Mainprise-King ('Dahti-Fahti'), a gentleman in the real sense of the word.

In the Japanese offensive of February 1944, of our four infantry company commanders, all young ECOs, none survived unscathed. Two were killed, and two (of whom I was one) were wounded. Not surprisingly, infantry companies had the highest casualties.

Additionally, we had a further four officers killed in the Arakan, three in a freak Japanese air attack on the 'Admin Box'. I am not certain of the details but understand that their deaths were caused by exploding ammunition and burning vehicles. They were the only casualties that we incurred, throughout the war, by enemy air action.

We also had serving at different times eight Indian officers, commissioned from the India Military Academy. One later became a Brigadier in the Pakistan Army. They all served with distinction.

*Chapter 6*


## EARLY DAYS IN THE BRITISH ARMY


I spent the autumn of 1946 in a training centre at Crowborough. It was one of those dreary Nissen hut* camps that had mushroomed all over wartime England. The winter was cold and the training we did seemed an utter waste of time. I missed my former Indian Battalion, with all its cheerful and lovable soldiers, and requested that I be allowed to return to India long enough to be with the Battalion when it was finally disbanded. No one could foresee that the following year India was to be given independence and in the process be torn asunder in a massive bloodbath. The Colonel of the Middlesex Regiment had a copy of my application and quite rightly was most displeased and tore it up. This did me little or no good.

In the beginning of 1947 I was delighted to receive a posting order to join the 1st Battalion The Middlesex Regiment at Iserlohn in north-west Germany, then a part of the British Army of the Rhine. The Battalion was a specialized one, equipped with machine guns and mortars, all carried in light armoured tracked vehicles. But first I had to complete a two-month machine-gun course at Netheravon near Salisbury. I dared not tell my mother that I was glad to be leaving England, with all its petty restrictions, for I knew how much she enjoyed having me based at home. I had had a good time in England, but it was insufficient compensation to make me want to stay.

This was the second year of Clement Attlee's Labour Government and fundamental changes were taking place in the social fabric of the country. It was not that I took exception to these, rather it was the lack of confidence and optimism that I found depressing.

---

* Cylindrical and made of corrugated iron.

The plain answer was that Britain was broke. Britons found it hard to understand how we as a major world power, victorious in war, could be bankrupt and have to go cap in hand to the Americans for an onerous loan.

In early summer I went by train to Harwich to board a ferry to the Hook of Holland and from there continued my journey by military train to Iserlohn, just south of Dortmund. We avoided some of the worst areas of devastation in the Ruhr around Duisburg and Wuppertal, but what I saw was horrifying enough. I had never seen such total destruction and it seemed unbelievable that German citizens were continuing to live amongst the rubble created by the Allied bombing. It was a shocking sight and I shuddered to think what it must have looked like at the time of the German surrender two years previously in 1945. When I arrived roads and streets had been cleared and normal utilities were working; furthermore American Marshall Aid had begun and the so-called 'European Recovery Plan' had started.*

Iserlohn seemed relatively undamaged. The Battalion occupied a large German barracks on the outskirts of the town and the Officers' Mess was in a requisitioned large private house in one of the main streets. Living conditions were good. Unlike the civilians living around us, we had plenty of food and drink. Most soldiers had only one wish: to get out of the Army as soon as possible. This made it difficult to maintain morale and discipline. My first commanding officer was a wealthy man, who was far more interested in his race-horses in England than in his soldiers. For long periods he would leave the Battalion in the charge of his second-in-command, who was, to say the least, an amusing philanderer. Luckily, there was a hard core of efficient officers, senior warrant officers and sergeants who *were* good. Fortune later took a hand, for the CO was replaced and the 2IC was moved on. In my spare time I rode in the various gymkhanas, becoming a regular member of the Battalion equestrian team, which achieved considerable success. We were lucky in having some first-class requisitioned horses and good German grooms. In the winter months there was excellent shooting, particularly for

* Monetary assistance given under American patronage and supervised by General Marshall of the USA.

pheasants, hare and roebuck, for the Germans were forbidden to shoot, even on their own land.

It was in the late summer that an event of the greatest importance and good fortune in my life took place. I fell in love with Corry Arends, a Dutch child search officer in the United Nations Relief and Rehabilitation Administration (UNRRA). As the advancing British forces moved through Holland into Germany in 1945, she had volunteered and been recruited for secretarial duties, as she was fluent in both English and German. It soon became apparent that with her language qualifications and personal qualities of sympathy and understanding she would make an ideal child search officer, whose job it was to locate and repatriate the many lost children from the countries that were occupied by Germany. Some of them had been placed in orphanages and some were with German families. Corry found herself at UNRRA HQ in the area of the 1st British Corps at Iserlohn, responsible for the region of the Ruhr. To do her job she was provided with a car and a Polish driver. She travelled widely, visiting, in particular, the various DP (displaced persons) camps.

Strange to say, we first met at a cricket match. It was not that she enjoyed cricket, in fact quite the contrary; she had been inveigled to come by her room-mate. My immediate problem was to get some form of transport in which we could go out and enjoy each other's company. I was lucky in being allowed to use an armoured scout car as so-called 'recreational transport'. It was extremely uncomfortable and there was only a narrow armoured slit in front through which I could see the road when I was driving. The front machine gun had been removed and Corry sat in the gunner's seat. Another problem was that I had to pay for the petrol and it did only seven miles to the gallon. I kept a pair of overalls for Corry's use in the vehicle to protect her clothes from getting covered in oil. I even had a camouflage net aboard, which I once erected at the Dortmund Officers' Club in order to conceal the vehicle from prying eyes. Corry entered into the spirit of the thing. In post-war Germany this sort of indulgent behaviour was overlooked.

As winter approached, the scout car became increasingly impossible to use and I purchased a brand-new Volkswagen from a brother-officer who was returning to England. These were being sold direct from the factory to members of the Forces for £110 each. I had painted on the front mudguard a skull and crossbones, being then completely ignorant of the fact that it was the insignia of the German SS Death's Head Division. This was obviously in the worst possible taste, but surprisingly nobody commented, except the Mess Sergeant, who asked me if I was a former member of Hitler's body-guard. Needless to say, the insignia was quickly erased.

One day, just before the tea interval in a cricket match, a jeep arrived in a cloud of dust and a breathless Mess corporal announced that the Mess was on fire. We abandoned the match and all scrambled back in whatever transport was available, to find that the top floor of the building was ablaze and the roof had collapsed. Our intrepid 2IC, who had just returned from seeing his mistress in Denmark, immediately took over command and went up to where the roof had been, only to have a small piece of burning wood fall on his head. With great *sang-froid* he called for his batman, Jones, to come to his aid. His batman arrived with a glass water jug on a tray. Turning to Jones he shouted, 'Jones, put me out!' Jones obliged by emptying the contents over the 2IC's head. By this time a crowd of German civilians had assembled in the road below; upon seeing the extraordinary sight of a soldier pouring a jug of water over an officer's head they burst into spontaneous cheering and clapping.

The fire was extinguished with the aid of two German fire engines, and to my amazement the 2IC decreed that we would have a formal dinner that evening to demonstrate our 'Diehard' spirit. (The Middlesex Regiment was known throughout the Army as the 'Diehards', a nickname earned at the battle of Albuhera during the Peninsular War.*)

In 1947 the German deutschmark was almost totally valueless and all Occupational Forces personnel were paid in BAFVS (British Army Forces Vouchers), which were in sterling currency. They were valid only in British organizations, with the result that all trading with the Germans was carried out in 'black market' currency: coffee, cigarettes and liquor. This was illegal, but proved impossible to stop.

It had been decided that the Officers' Mess was to hold a presti-gious party in the late autumn. The CO excused me from all military duties for six weeks before the party in order to make all the

---

* A battle fought against the French in Spain, 1811.

necessary arrangements. The party was to take place in the Iserlohn Officers' Club and no expense was to be spared. Invitations had been sent to Princess Elizabeth and Prince Philip (the invitation, not surprisingly, was declined). I was also asked to arrange a cabaret, which was to include the best girl crooner in Germany, Margot Tischmann, a good striptease artiste (but I had to inspect her feathers), a well-known caricaturist from Holland and a conjuror. The Band and Corps of Drums of the Regiment were also to perform in their full-dress scarlet uniforms.

The CO said that I could use his staff car whenever I wanted; he also wanted me to go to Belgium to arrange for a delivery of oysters. Additionally, I was to organize a pheasant and duck shoot on the General's private shoot near a place called Emmerich on the Rhine, in order to provide some of the food. What we shot was to be hung in the town mortuary by arrangement with the Town Major, an army officer working for what was known as the Control Commission Germany (CCG) (I never asked what was to happen to the corpses that might be in normal occupation of the mortuary). I remonstrated that I was probably the last person who should be asked to organize such a party, for I had lived a fairly spartan life during my soldiering days in India and Burma, and therefore had not had the opportunity to attend any prestigious social events. The CO replied that, as I had had the privilege of being educated at a public school, I must therefore be capable of organizing a party such as this. It was impossible to deal with such a man.

In the event the party was an outstanding success and some 300 guests enjoyed themselves. The only major mishap was that the striptease artiste got drunk, forgot her feathers and tried to perform in the nude. I expected to be asked to resign my commission.

Corry had returned to Holland in the autumn, for her job had in the main been completed and the role of UNRRA had been taken over by the International Relief Organization (IRO). In November the Battalion moved to Hamburg, not far from the border with the Soviet Occupied Zone. I missed Corry terribly and took every opportunity to go to Holland in my primitive Volkswagen, embodying the minimum of comfort, to see her. The journey across battle-scarred northern Germany was far from easy, particularly as I travelled at night and signposting was very poor. Seeing her and her large friendly family compensated for everything. It was always a

wonderful change to cross the border into Holland and find friend-
liness, order and cleanliness after the dreadful squalor of Germany.
I have vivid memories of the roads in Eindhoven, where Corry's
family lived, jammed with bicycles when the Philips Electrical facto-
ries stopped work, and thinking that on Sundays every person in the
Catholic south must be going to church: the numerous churches
were packed for every Mass.

Corry's family lived in a large, spacious house on the outskirts of
Eindhoven. Both her father and her youngest brother had been
imprisoned for six months by the Germans for distributing information prepared by the Dutch Underground Movement. They were
kept with others as hostages to be taken out and shot as reprisals
for wrongdoing by the Dutch, such as pushing German soldiers
into canals where there was no way out. Their imprisonment
added considerably to the worries of the family under the German
occupation.

In March 1948 Corry and I became officially engaged, not quite
knowing when we would get married. The wedding date was finally
decided for us when the Battalion was ordered to return to England
in June 1948. It was kindly fixed that I could remain in Germany
for a short while and then take a month's leave in Holland and
England.

We were first married in an obligatory civil ceremony at the Town
Hall in Eindhoven on 22 July 1948, and then five days later in St
Theresia Catholic Church, Eindhoven. The wedding procedures
were very different from those in England; they lasted for the major
part of the day and most of the evening. After the Nuptial Mass, all
close relations returned to Corry's parents' house for a wedding
breakfast. This in turn was followed by a reception at which Corry
and I received well-wishers. In the evening there was a splendid
formal dinner, held in a local hall, involving various speeches, other
forms of entertainment and dancing. Corry and I finally left well
after midnight, to motor to nearby Vught, where we were to spend
our wedding night in a hotel on a lake, only to find that it was so
late the place was shut. After some commotion we finally managed
to arouse the manager of the hotel, who appeared at an upstairs
window in his nightshirt and agreed to let us in.

My best man was an old Indian Army friend, David Eales, who
had served in the Jat Regiment in the Indian Army and, like me, had

joined the Middlesex Regiment. He had two notable distinguishing features: his back had been badly scarred by a tiger, which had attacked him in India when he was shooting peafowl; and he was tattooed on his forearm as the result of a drunken bet. He later became ADC to the Governor of the Sudan, but was forced to leave after killing a Sudanese boy while driving one of the Governor's Rolls Royces. David later went to do a year's course in Arabic at the Middle East Centre of Arabic Studies in Beirut, and eventually became a military adviser to a Sheikh in one of the Gulf States. He came to a sad and untimely end when he was shot by his Arab orderly while asleep in his tent. The motive for the murder was never disclosed. He was a good friend and a most unusual man.

It was in June that war clouds had once again appeared on the horizon, for the Russians under Stalin cut all land communications from the West to Berlin, which was then controlled under quadri-partite agreement by the Americans, British, French and Russians. This action resulted in the Western sector being entirely supplied by air for the next eleven months. Many of us thought it likely that we could find ourselves at war with Russia.

## Return to England

Corry and I returned to England soon after our wedding. The Battalion was now stationed at Inglis Barracks at Mill Hill in north London. No quarters were available and initially we stayed at my mother's flat in London. We had little money; my net monthly pay totalled the princely sum of £65, which had to cover everything, including the upkeep of my uniform and mess bill. We certainly could not afford to run a car.

The big event of the summer in 1948 was the holding of the Olympic Games in England. It was the first and only time that the Games have been held in England. We managed to obtain tickets for the England v. India hockey match, and also got tickets for the spectacular final day's events, when we saw England win a gold medal in the Equestrian Team Jumping.

Later in 1948 the Battalion moved from Mill Hill to Chelsea Barracks and took over guard duties at Buckingham Palace. Corry and I moved to a small flat in a private house just outside the barrack gates at Mill Hill; it was our first home and we were very proud of it. From a military viewpoint this period was boring in the extreme, consisting of almost continual drill and guard-mounting practices, and it did the Battalion no good at all to be in the centre of London with very few training and recreational facilities.

There was a custom in the Regiment that all regular commissioned officers should be initiated as Diehards. The rites were secret and carried out in all solemnity by the Commanding Officer. It involved the swearing of an oath and a so-called 'ordeal by fire'. The rite always took place following a formal 'dinner night' in a secure room, lit only by candlelight. It had its origins in the latter part of the nineteenth century and must have been based in part on certain Masonic rites. Nobody would divulge what was entailed, so I approached my own initiation with some apprehension. In the event I found the whole thing anachronistic and something of an anticlimax. Years later, when commanding the same Battalion, I in turn became responsible for conducting the same rites, but I did succeed, with the approval of the Colonel of the Regiment, in simplifying the procedure and eliminating the 'ordeal by fire'.

In March 1949 Pieter-John (P.J.), our first son, was born (feet first) at Edgware Hospital. He was ten weeks premature and weighed only 3 lb 4 oz. It was a miracle that he survived. Corry had to stay in hospital until the baby weighed 5 lb, which took a long time. P.J.'s arrival coincided with the news that in June the Battalion was to move to Hong Kong for an indefinite tour of duty. This was worrying news for us and we decided that, once the baby was fit and well, Corry would return to her family in Eindhoven and await developments.

The decision to reinforce the Hong Kong garrison by approximately one division was taken because of reports that Chinese Communist troops were massing south of Canton near the Hong Kong border with the intention of seizing both Hong Kong Island and the British Leased Territories on the Kowloon peninsular. Chinese Communist forces led by the famed Mao Tse-tung had already defeated the Chinese Nationalists under General Chiang Kai-shek. The Communists' future intentions were far from clear, but in October, just three months after our arrival, Mao Tse-tung established the Chinese Peoples' Republic throughout mainland China.

## Voyage to Hong Kong

In June the Battalion embarked at Southampton on the troopship *Dunera*. I did not know when and where I would see Corry and P.J. again; we were both equally anxious about the future.

The *Dunera* was not a large ship, being only 12,600 tons with a top speed of 14 knots. Our voyage took just over four weeks, passing through the Suez Canal, Aden and Trincomalee in Ceylon (now Sri Lanka). I had covered much of this route in the reverse direction only two years earlier when I returned home from Singapore. I little thought then that I would be returning to the Far East after such a short space of time.

The voyage to Hong Kong was peaceful and enjoyable, for there was time to relax and shake off the problems of departure before encountering the new challenges that lay ahead. For all we knew, we might soon be involved in a futile war against Chinese Communist forces intent upon capturing Hong Kong. The voyage was rather like being in a state of limbo. In later years all military moves have been carried out by air and troopships have become a thing of the past. With air travel one has hardly said goodbye, eaten a packed meal and drunk a few cups of coffee before the plane is landing at its destination, possibly thousands of miles away, leaving its occupants feeling tired and jaded to face new problems in an entirely different environment. If there is a choice give me sea travel any day.

It was fun to go exploring in Port Said once again and be accosted by the numerous touts and pimps:

'Sahib, you want buy feelthy postcard? You come with me, I show.'

'You want nice white woman, all pink and fat like Queen Victoria?'

In Aden we had the opportunity to go ashore. I was following in the footsteps of my grandfather and father, who had been there so many times in years gone by when voyaging to and from Australia and Burma. Then we sailed on to Trincomalee, where some of us spent a pleasant day lunching with regimental friends stationed there. Finally, there was the great excitement of sailing into the magnificent harbour of Hong Kong, situated between Hong Kong Island with its dominating Victoria Peak (1,780 feet high) and the Kowloon Peninsula.

# Hong Kong

The name Hong Kong has its derivation from the Chinese word *hiang kiang* meaning 'good harbour'. The island was ceded to Britain by the Chinese in 1842 and the New Territories on the main land were leased to Britain for 99 years in 1898. Today both Hong Kong and the New Territories have been returned to China. In the nineteenth century Hong Kong was the centre for the flourishing opium trade (known to the Chinese as 'foreign mud'), carried on by British trading companies, much to their discredit.

Our arrival unfortunately coincided with the middle of the monsoon period, with its torrential rain and high humidity. We were, however, lucky to be quartered in some old barracks on the island at Lye Mun, which overlooked the harbour at its narrowest point with the mainland. The thing that made the most immediate impression on me was the cleanliness and orderliness of the Chinese. Although Hong Kong itself was overcrowded – Chinese families were sometimes living six or eight in one room, and many thousands were living in makeshift shelters on the outskirts of both Hong Kong and Kowloon – there was a strong impression of industry and purpose. There had at this time been a great influx of Chinese from the mainland, escaping from Communist China. In 1949 the population of the whole Colony was approximately 1 million; today it is over 5 million. It was incredible that so many Chinese refugees had found sufficient space in which to live. The answer lies in the enormous increase in high-rise buildings.

Other things that impressed me on arrival were the numerous *sampans*; these were small light boats, propelled by a single oar, on which whole families would frequently live. Within the harbour and along the coastline stately-looking junks with their distinctive high stern and lug sails made of matting plied their way. Hong Kong looked particularly beautiful at night, with its myriad of lights and flashing neon signs, while in the harbour both naval and civilian ships were illuminated and many were 'dressed overall' (decorated with coloured lights and bunting from bow to stern). In the city there was continual noise and activity throughout the night, resembling an antheap working non-stop.

Very soon after our arrival we learned of a dramatic incident involving the Royal Navy frigate HMS *Amethyst*. In April 1949 *Amethyst* had been sent from Shanghai up the Yangtze River to deliver mail and stores to the beleaguered British Embassy in Nanking, some 180 miles up the river. She was caught between the opposing Communist and Nationalist forces and was fired at by the Communists, when some 140 miles from the sea, damaging the ship and killing the Captain and seventeen of the crew. Commander Kerens, who was at the British Embassy in Nanking, was allowed by the Communists to come aboard to take command. For nearly three months the *Amethyst* had been moored in the Yangtze River covered by Communist guns and denied fuel. She was permitted to take on board only limited supplies of fresh food.

On 30 July the *Amethyst* slipped her moorings, made a 180 degree turn and, under heavy gunfire, made the 140 mile dash to the open sea. Despite being hit, she successfully navigated the narrow shoals in the river and on 3 August reached Hong Kong. Excitement was at fever pitch among both the European and Chinese population. When the *Amethyst* finally reached Hong Kong she was given a tumultuous welcome. Every ship in the harbour sounded its foghorn and the naval ships fired a salute. The Battalion provided a full guard of honour at the Naval Dockyard. It was one of the most exciting events that I have ever witnessed and it deservedly captured press attention throughout the world. Commander Kerens was awarded an immediate DSO and a very successful film was made of the whole incident. He said afterwards:

> I was treated with the utmost discourtesy. Everything was thrown at me. I was subjected to personal vilification for weeks on end. They even threatened me with the destruction of my ship.

Later in August the Battalion moved from Hong Kong Island to the New Territories on the mainland, first to a tented camp at Sek Kong where a new airfield was being built and then later close to the Chinese border, where the majority of the Battalion was accommodated in requisitioned racing stables near Fanling. Our time was fully spent on training exercises and on practising contingency plans in the event of a Chinese incursion, or, worse still, an all-out assault by land, sea and air. It was pretty obvious to everyone that the Colony could not be defended against a determined attack for any length of time. First, the area was too small to allow any defence in depth; second, our two airfields could easily be neutralized; and third, the main water reservoirs were situated in the New Territories, and if they were captured, Hong Kong would be without water.

Sometimes the thought crossed my mind that we might be going to repeat the experience of eight years previously, when Japanese forces invaded from the mainland in the last week of 1941. The 1st Battalion then had the grim task of taking part in the hopeless defence of Hong Kong. The fighting lasted for seventeen days and nights, and ended on Christmas Day. The Battalion fought with the greatest tenacity, suffering over 200 casualties, and gained the admiration of all who came in contact with it, including, surprisingly, the Japanese. After ten months some 1,800 prisoners were shipped by the Japanese from Hong Kong to Japan in a ship called the *Lisbon Maru*, which unfortunately was torpedoed by an American submarine, unaware that her cargo was prisoners of war. The Japanese locked everyone in the holds and fired on those who attempted to escape. The calm courage of the Commanding Officer, Colonel 'Monkey' Stewart, prevented panic; he organized the breaking open of the hatches and thus managed to save 900 men from the sea. On arrival in Japan Colonel Stewart survived for only a few days, worn out by 'his exertions on behalf of his beloved men and from the knowledge of the cruel fate of so many'. He was awarded a posthumous DSO. There were still in the Battalion a small number of survivors from the long years of captivity in Japan. It seemed to me to be wrong that they should find themselves back in Hong Kong with a possible further battle, but they all had volunteered to remain.

In October the Chinese forces closed right up to the border and an attack seemed imminent. Colonel Andrew Man, who had just arrived to take over command, describes how two days after his arrival the Brigade Commander, Basil Coad, told him: 'We expect the Chinese to attack tomorrow. I will not give you any order which I would not be prepared to carry out myself. Good luck.' We trained hard by day and by night on the hills overlooking China and slowly the threat of an invasion diminished.

A group of Nationalist soldiers had occupied a small island called Tsing Yi in the Canton River estuary and the Communists were trying to dislodge them. An old Marlborough friend, Richard Corfield, was then flying Auster light reconnaissance aircraft and offered to take me, unofficially, to see the fighting. I readily accepted, but we violated the Chinese border, which created quite a rumpus, and resulted in Richard's being reprimanded and my having to see the Divisional Commander, General Evans, who, fortunately, had been my Divisional Commander in Burma and knew me well, so the incident passed off relatively easily.

In early 1950 life started to resume a more normal pattern and the Chinese threat began to evaporate. I put in an application for Corry and P.J. to join me in Hong Kong. The application was granted provided that I could find accommodation. I managed to get a room-cum-sitting room in a Chinese-run hotel in Kowloon, sharing a balcony with a Chinese family. Corry returned to England from Holland and in March embarked on the troopship *Empire Hallidale*, arriving in Hong Kong in mid-April after a five-week voyage. It had been far from easy for her travelling alone with a small baby. Naturally, we were thrilled to see each other again, but the living conditions were bad and would not be tolerated today.

We made the best of things and purchased a decrepit old car through a dishonest officer. We later discovered that it had started life as a taxi; it had then been used as a private car, had been stolen and finally had been dumped in the harbour, fished out and 'made good'. It was a death-trap on wheels. On one occasion the front wheel came off and passed us on the road; it had rusted away. On another occasion the steering system collapsed. To add to the hazards of driving, the local Chinese had a habit of sometimes deliberately running out in front of a car; the idea was that the car would miss them but kill an evil spirit that they thought was dogging their footsteps.

One day I was driving to Kowloon with my Company Sergeant Major, CSM Wild, when we both noticed that a Chinese riding a motorcycle in front of us had a revolver strapped to a belt on his backside. It could be clearly seen when the wind caught his shirt. We thought he was a bandit and decided to apprehend him. In the busy streets of Kowloon more and more people wishing to rid themselves of evil spirits jumped out in front of us, narrowly escaping death. We continually had to brake hard and nearly lost our quarry, but managed to get a glimpse of him turning off to Kai Tak, the main airfield, where there was a police station. We informed the police, who said that they would establish a roadblock on the road ahead. I followed the bandit, but eventually lost him in some hilly country, for my old car was not up to the chase. On returning to Kai Tak police station I was surprised to see our bandit chatting amiably to a group of policemen. CSM Wild laughingly told me that we had been following a police inspector in plain clothes.

After a few weeks Corry and I managed to improve our living conditions by moving into a better hotel on the harbour front in Kowloon, but again the three of us had to live and sleep in one room. It was here that P.J. developed whooping cough, which was terribly worrying. The weather was very hot and sticky, and of course there was no air-conditioning. At night our bedroom underwent a regular invasion of cockroaches. We tried to combat them with various forms of trap, including discarded gin and tonic glasses baited with water in which our victims would drown, and insecticides, but nothing seemed to work. We were forced to accept them as a normal part of our life. The redeeming factor of the room was that it had a fairly large balcony. Overall we managed to enjoy ourselves, with the aid of our rickety car and help from a Chinese *amah* (nurse) by the name of Ah Seng.

The highlight of these early months in Hong Kong was a two-day visit by boat to Macau in late July. This old Portuguese colony, founded in 1557, was the first European trading outpost on the coast of China, and lies about 40 miles from Hong Kong. The place had a distinct and charming decadent air of past grandeur and was dominated by its large catholic cathedral. At the time of our visit Macau had a reputation for gambling and also for its numerous brothels. Corry felt unwell, as she had just become pregnant again, so she was not able to see as much as she would have liked. I, however, visited a gambling saloon, and in company with local Chinese played *fan-tan*, a Chinese game not unlike roulette. I had been given an 'infallible system' by an army Catholic padre in Hong Kong and, much to my amazement, won a fair amount of money, which I immediately converted into purchases of clothing and Portuguese wine. Corry remembers Macau best for the continuous clinking clatter made by the ivory and bone pieces of mahjong sets, used seemingly by the whole population for gambling. Mahjong is one of the oldest Chinese games; it originated over 1,000 years ago. The game was once very popular in England and we still have my parents' Mahjong set complete with all its carved bone pieces, like small dominoes.

*Chapter 7*


# INTO ACTION IN KOREA*


During the early morning of 25 June 1950 the North Korean Army crossed the 38th Parallel on the Korean peninsula to invade South Korea. The South Korean Army was poorly organized and consisted of some eight so-called divisions. It had no artillery, armour or air support. The attack was ruthlessly carried out, and Seoul, the capital, fell five days later. The few battalions of American infantry located in South Korea as occupational forces were the first to meet the onslaught. They were, generally speaking, both badly trained and equipped. The world watched in dismay as American forces were compelled to retreat. The United States' bridgehead in the south grew smaller and smaller, and many thought that the port of Pusan might soon be remembered as a Far East Dunkirk. The first American reinforcement units to arrive in Korea went into action on 4 July, but it was not until the middle of July that American troops arrived in considerable strength. By then the North Koreans had advanced some 90 miles south of Seoul. In early August the situation was desperate and all territory west of the Naktong River was in North Korean hands.


---

* In writing these Korean reminiscences I have relied largely on *The Diehards in Korea* which I edited and had printed, complete with maps and photographs, in 1975. Brigadier Basil Coad, then a Major General, very kindly wrote a Foreword, and Colonel Andrew Man added his reminiscences for good measure. The contents were based on anonymous articles written during the war and sent back to England on a regular basis for publication in our regimental magazine. I am indebted to the author or authors of those articles.

## The Korean War

Japan had previously occupied Korea (1904); after their eviction at the end of World War II the country was divided. The Russians armed the North and the Americans moved into the South. The North Korean invasion was motivated by territorial aggression and encouraged by Russia, who wanted the important airfields in the south from which they could better neutralize the threat imposed by the Americans in Japan. At the time nobody explained these strategic implications. Quite simply I looked on the war as necessary to get rid of the North Koreans. The reality was that I disliked all Koreans on account of their cruelty, when working as guards, to our prisoners in Japan and on the Burmese railway.

Both Koreans and Japanese have their origins within the large Mongol family and have similar physical characteristics. Their countries are large rice producers and rice forms part of their staple diet. The ricefields are ubiquitous in both countries.

This was the first United Nations war and many countries throughout the world contributed to the ground, air and naval forces, all under American command. The predominant contribution was, of course, American. In the few months that I was there we fought alongside Australian infantry and were supported by New Zealand gunners and an Indian Field Ambulance Company. We also had contact with a Turkish infantry battalion.

The war was to last approximately three years, with an armistice signed between the Americans and Chinese (who by that time had entered the war) in July 1953 at, ironically, the 38th Parallel, which was where the war began. American casualties amounted to 140,000, of whom 37,000 were killed, but the biggest sufferers were the South Koreans, whose casualties totalled over 800,000, of whom about half were killed. By comparison British and Commonwealth casualties were light, totalling 6,000, but then our forces were small.* In the late summer of 1950 all our hopes were centred on a quick end to the war and no one could envisage the slaughter and hardship which lay ahead.

* Max Hastings, *The Korean War* (London: Michael Joseph, 1987).

Peace talks finally culminated in the signing of an Armistice at Panmunjong on 27 July 1953, guaranteeing the integrity of South Korea. It was, in the opinion of Max Hastings, 'a struggle that the West was right to fight', for, by its victory, it ensured the future integrity of South Korea.

In early August the Prime Minister, Clement Attlee, made a statement that no troops were to be sent to Korea from Hong Kong, but politicians have been known to change their minds. Corry and I were beginning to enjoy our stay in Hong Kong to the full when suddenly, at 9 a.m. on Sunday 20 August, our Brigade Headquarters told Colonel Man that our Battalion and the 1st Battalion the Argyll and Sutherland Highlanders would be sailing from Hong Kong for Korea in five days' time in the aircraft carrier HMS *Unicorn* and the cruiser HMS *Ceylon*. That left only four days in which to draw up stores, pack and prepare in every way. The urgency precluded time for disbelief. After only four months together Corry and I were facing separation again. Corry could have decided to return to England at the first opportunity, but as the future was so uncertain she decided to stay on and stick it out. This was not easy for her with one small boy and now expecting another baby, living in one room in a very modest Chinese hotel. It was also not easy for me to leave for Korea, an unknown place, and a war 1,300 miles away.


## Arrival in Korea

I had been detailed to fly to Japan en route for Korea with the Battalion advance party for which I was responsible. John Slim, the son of Field Marshal Slim, was responsible for the Argylls' advance party. We left Hong Kong from Kai Tak airfield in a US Air Force plane. Corry came to see me off. We kidded each other that we were going to Japan merely to 'show the flag'. We spent our first night at a US Air Force base in Japan, where we had our initial introduction to 'Americanization'. We went to our evening meal carrying our mess tins and proceeded under a bamboo archway proclaiming: 'The God damndest fighting pilots in the world go down this chow line'. We spent the latter part of the evening in the Officers' Club, drank too much and spent an inordinate amount of time explaining to disbelieving American wives that the Jocks (Scottish soldiers) really did wear nothing under their kilts: 'Oh gee, do they really have nothing on under their skirts?'

The next day we flew to Taegu, which was included in the Pusan bridgehead. It was an unexpected introduction to the war, as the airfield was under intermittent artillery fire. I surprised some of the Americans by alighting from the aircraft with golf clubs and tennis racquet, which I later had to abandon on the perimeter of the airfield. When I departed from Hong Kong I had been firmly convinced that our final destination was to be a comfortable location in Japan and was advised to take recreational items: hence my golf clubs and tennis racquet. After my return from Korea I submitted an insurance claim for the loss of my golf clubs. The insurance company replied that I was not covered under the terms of the policy, but as the claim was such an unusual one and the circumstances so bizarre, their Board had decided to pay me twice the sum I had claimed.

After the war was over Eric Linklater, the noted author and historian, wrote:

> Our land forces were small in material strength but were endowed with all the aptitude of their calling and that tenacity of spirit which is traditional in the British Army. Neither the Diehards nor the Argylls could muster more than three rifle companies, and there was no military principle to justify the despatch and committing to battle of two weak battalions that had neither their own necessary transport nor their proper supporting arms. It was the desperate plight of the Americans in the Pusan bridgehead that had compelled their sudden embarkation, and, as military principles were overridden by moral need, so were the difficulties of their strange campaigning to be overcome by recruitment, as it seemed, from the regimental spirit to which they were the heirs. In the months to come both The Middlesex and The Argylls – though nearly half of them were youngsters doing their National Training – were to enhance the pride and reputation, not only of The Diehards and The Argylls, but of all the Army.

The whole Battalion assembled in an area some 60 miles north of Pusan. We were now an integral part of the 27th Commonwealth Brigade along with the Argylls and later the 3rd Royal Australian

Regiment. The weather was superb, with a warm sun by day and a nice nip in the air by night. A stream that ran through the area provided a ready-made cold bath. Apple orchards were heavy with bright red fruit and one evening I discovered a large and busy beehive in a deserted Korean village. We smoked the bees out with a smoke grenade, took out the waxen combs and sieved the honey through a mosquito net. There was enough for the whole of my company.

One of the more exciting events at this time was receiving American stores, rations and vehicles. The item that aroused the most interest was the individual 'C' Ration, which was extremely good, but became somewhat monotonous with the passing of time. Everyone receiving his first issue behaved like a small boy at Christmas opening his stocking to see what Santa Claus had brought him. Each ration contained: three tins of a main meal, such as chicken and vegetables, ham and lima beans, meat hash, or frankfurter and beans; three tins of crackers (dry biscuits); cookies (sweet biscuits); candy; separate packets of instant coffee and sugar; two boxes of matches; 20 American cigarettes.

The war seemed far away, but it was brought closer by the thousands of Korean refugees who streamed south on every available track or path. They were pathetic figures carrying their meagre possessions, tied to wooden frames on their backs or, if lucky, moving their belongings in large wooden ox-carts. I wondered what fighting with British soldiers would be like, for my only combat experience had been with the Indian Army. I also thought about how I would react under fire, having already been wounded three times in Burma. I soon discovered that my fears were groundless. The humour and goodwill of our soldiers carried us along during the months ahead and the excitement and tensions allowed no time for introspection.


## Into Action

Our days of peace were short-lived; after a few days we moved to take up defensive positions on the Naktong River alongside the US 1st Cavalry Division. By 1 September North Korean forces had crossed the river in seventeen places, but that was to be the high water mark of their success. It was on the Naktong that we had our

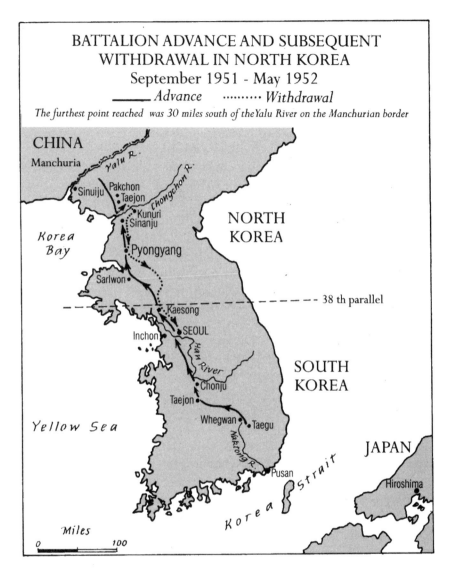

## BATTALION ADVANCE AND SUBSEQUENT WITHDRAWAL IN NORTH KOREA
### September 1951 - May 1952
_____ Advance    ·········· Withdrawal

*The furthest point reached was 30 miles south of the Yalu River on the Manchurian border*

CHINA

Manchuria

*Yalu R.*

Sinuiju
Pakchon
Taejon
*Chongchon R.*
Kunuri
Sinanju

NORTH
KOREA

Korea
Bay

Pyongyang

Sariwon

— — — — — — 38 th parallel

Kaesong
SEOUL
Inchon

Han River

SOUTH
KOREA

Chonju
Taejon

Whegwan   Taegu

Yellow Sea

Naktong R.

JAPAN

Pusan   Korea Strait

Hiroshima

Miles
0               100

first casualties, and killed our first North Koreans. A young platoon commander in my Company (Chris Lawrence) earned the first Military Cross of the war for seizing an important enemy position.

This period is most memorable for my seeing at close quarters a disaster of major proportions. The Argylls had put in an attack on a hill feature to our left. This attack was successful and they laid out fluorescent air-panels to identify themselves to American strike aircraft. There was a tragic misunderstanding and the attacking

121

planes dropped napalm right on top of the Argylls' position, covering them in a living sheet of flame. There were over 100 casualties from severe burns and many were burnt alive. We all gave what assistance we could, but our immediate medical resources were woefully inadequate. This incident left a great sense of shock throughout the Brigade, and I wondered whether the Argylls might become inoperative. However, some of the injuries proved to be superficial and a few days later the Argylls, although depleted in strength, were once again in action and fighting hard with their usual good humour. The Argylls' Second-in-Command, Major Kenny Muir, was killed in the aftermath of the napalm attack. He was awarded a posthumous Victoria Cross for his gallantry.*

After various minor moves we finally crossed the Naktong River. One morning, when walking to Battalion Headquarters, I was greeted with incredulous stares. I asked what was up and was told that I had been reported killed. The headless body of a British officer had, so rumour had it, been found near our crossing place, and as I was known to be in the area it was reported as being me. It was certainly not one of our officers; I never discovered who it was.

## Pursuit

Later in September General MacArthur, the Supreme Commander, with his Headquarters in Japan, carried out a seaborne landing at Inchon, some 220 miles to the north. The landing was virtually unopposed and a complete success. The North Koreans fighting in the South were wrong-footed and their Army disintegrated. Soldiers threw away their weapons and uniforms and tried to disguise themselves in civilian clothes. We were ordered to return to Taegu and fly north to Seoul, the capital of South Korea. I was fortunate in moving by road and was therefore able to see the extent of the North Korean defeat. All along the appalling, dusty roads were abandoned tanks and trucks and the usual debris of war. Frequently we would pass an area that had been the target for a napalm attack; here the places would be littered with burnt or partly burnt bodies and

* There were only four Victoria Crosses awarded throughout the Korean War.

the sweet sickly stench of decomposition was nauseating. It is disturbing how easily I accepted these dreadful sights; these charred remains were once ordinary people like myself. In many ways it was reminiscent of my fairly recent experiences in Burma.

Our road took us through numerous small towns and villages, most of which had been totally destroyed by the United States Air Force. One particular event stuck in my mind. While travelling at night our convoy came to a complete halt. I walked up the road and found that a wooden bridge had partly collapsed. In the small gully below the bridge an overturned ox-cart lay, loaded with family possessions. The ox lay on its side, still in the shafts, and a small family group were wailing in the darkness. We helped them up onto the road and gave them some food, but sadly there was little else we could do. Some hours later we moved on. I often thought about them and wondered where they had come from, where they were going and what future lay in store for them with virtually everything lost.

Seoul was recaptured on 26 September and General MacArthur, the Supreme United Nations Commander, accompanied by President Syngman Rhee, the South Korean President, entered the city the same day. Our road journey to Seoul, of some 225 miles, took four days. Progress was slow because American air attacks had destroyed numerous bridges; also there were large numbers of refugees moving both north and south. We passed many abandoned North Korean tanks and vehicles that had been destroyed by air attacks using napalm.

Seoul was a city of the dead. The only non-military transport to be seen was ox-carts. On one particular visit I saw a large number of men, women and children being marched along, tied together with ropes, escorted by South Korean soldiers. I failed to find out what was happening to them, but I suspected that they had been classed as collaborators and that in a few hours they would all be shot.

The abrupt transformation of the campaign was the result of the successful seaborne attack on Inchon and of the efforts of the United States 8th Army, who had turned defence into attack. The political dilemma after the fall of Seoul was whether to continue the pursuit into North Korea or halt on the 38th Parallel. General MacArthur decided on pursuit and on 1 October South Korean troops crossed the Parallel. Our Battalion crossed on 11 October in company with the 1st Cavalry Division – 'General Hobart Gay's Own'. There was a large painted sign by the roadside proclaiming 'You are crossing the 38th Parallel by courtesy of General Hobart Gay's Own', accompanied by a yellow badge with the distinctive horse's head. This badge was to become very familiar in the weeks ahead. We added our own suitably worded message from the Diehards welcoming all-comers to North Korea. Amongst graffiti by the roadside mention must be made of Kilroy, a character who remained with the Battalion on its travels. Kilroy is a legendary figure of the American soldier (GI), a character indistinguishable from any one American soldier, yet identifiable with all. One of the signs that we put up by the roadside proclaimed in large letters:

THE MIDS CAN SAY WITH GLEE AND JOY
THAT THEY WERE HERE BEFORE KILROY.

An endless stream of tanks and vehicles was now heading north towards Pyongyang, the capital of North Korea, driving through choking clouds of yellow dust and burnt villages. Overhead an endless stream of aircraft was going, in American parlance, to 'knock the hammers of shit out of those North Korean gooks'. Everywhere there was a feeling of euphoria. We felt that the war had been won and that with any luck we would be home by Christmas.

On 17 October the Argylls entered Sariwon, a town about 50 miles to the south of Pyongyang. It was here that two escape routes for the North Koreans converged. Fighting went on throughout the night; when we reached the place dead Koreans were everywhere and the Scots were, of course, jubilant. I was met in Sariwon by our Second-in-Command, Major Roly Gwyn, who told me that a Korean field hospital had been captured, including a number of Korean nurses, all of whom were being well looked after. A paymaster unit had also been captured, including many heavy reinforced boxes containing vast sums of money. He gave me one large box packed with millions of Korean wan. My jeep-driver and signaller were convinced that we would be set up for life. I asked them what we should do with the money and we came to a democratic decision that the best thing to do was to buy a chicken and some eggs. We soon discovered that the local villagers had no chickens to sell and only with some difficulty did we buy a few eggs for half a million wan. Inflation had already taken its toll; the money was worthless. The box was far too heavy to cart around and we eventually threw it away with the money still inside it.

Just before we reached Sariwon our Brigade Commander told us that the Brigade would be leading the advance to Pyongyang and then onwards to the Manchurian border. Our advance from Sariwon soon developed into one enormous traffic jam, punctuated by short encounters with enemy rearguards. Three divisions were racing each other to be the first to enter Pyongyang in noisy, dusty nose-to-tail columns. The flurry of competition caused an extraordinary situation in which friend and foe were alike elbowed aside by impatient formations. At one period it was even necessary to block the road with one of our anti-tank guns to allow us to take our designated place in the order of march. Pressure from behind allowed no time to mop up, nor to destroy the great quantities of abandoned enemy equipment and weapons that littered the countryside. It is an exciting and invigorating experience to participate in a full-scale pursuit of a beaten enemy. Perhaps these primitive feelings have their origins in man's early background as a hunter.

On 26 October, when only 21 miles from Pyongyang, the Battalion led the advance but was seriously delayed by diversions due to mine clearance. We eventually got into the suburbs of the city only to find that some South Korean troops had got there first. Just outside Pyongyang an American general stopped his jeep to ask me what arrangements were being made for a ceremonial parade on entry to the city. He was not accompanied by any staff, nor did he have any communications. Sitting on the seat beside him was what looked like a pedigree spaniel dog. Heaven knows who he thought I was. There certainly was no ceremonial entry.

## Rolling On

Each company had under its command five Patton tanks. The leading platoon rode on the tanks and the remainder of the company followed in trucks. For control the company commander had a choice of riding either in his jeep or on the tank commander's tank (our radios worked on different frequencies from those of the Americans).

When everyone was ready to move, and a measure of agreement had been reached as to which was the right route, the order 'Wind 'em up' was given. Every vehicle then backfired as it started, and the little army proceeded to roll along the road until it was shot at. Then almost anything could happen, and often did. One of the most remarkable things about this type of advance was the complete lack of information about destroyed bridges, the condition of roads, or engineer support available. The whole advance was carried out on an improvised, self-help basis. On one occasion half the battalion had crossed a ford and disappeared into the night while the rear half was left to fend for itself and carried out a bridging operation on its own.

I cannot recollect what Pyongyang looked like, for early the next morning we 'rolled on', heading for Sinanju on the Chongchon River, 50 miles to the north. The same day a brigade of the 82nd Airborne Division was dropped 20 miles ahead of us. Nobody had informed us and it came as a complete surprise to meet paratroopers marching towards us. At the time that we made contact my company was leading. It was an exciting and heart-warming experience. The paratroops had been expecting a fight and their relief was obvious, for they were full of good humour, waving North Korean flags and some wearing Korean hats. We reached the Chongchon River the following day to find the large road girder bridge down; spasmodic shelling from Russian T34 tanks and SU76 self-propelled guns was coming from the far bank.

Winter was now approaching in earnest and the cold winds were starting to blow down from Siberia. In forward positions slit trenches were packed with rice straw in order to keep out the cold and on the reverse slopes of hills camp-fires were lit. It was even reported that the bare fingers of soldiers had been frozen to the steel sides of vehicles. The worst part of the cold was the cruelty of the Siberian winds, but neither the wind nor the cold seemed to daunt our soldiers. They had no comfort and were living in frozen holes in the ground. The first icy blasts arrived one night and sleep was impossible. At this time we were still wearing the summer uniforms that we had in Hong Kong. Proper winter clothing was, however, soon at hand and we were issued with parkas, thick khaki pullovers and string vests. Graphite grease was also made available to prevent our weapons from freezing up. Despite having anti-freeze for our vehicles, we also had to take the precaution of frequently running the engines to prevent them from freezing up. We had to risk the noise at night or we might run the penalty of losing our mobility. A few weeks later, when I was drinking tea, my lips momentarily froze to my mess tin. The greatest luxury was to have the opportunity to spend the night in a Korean house; most of them had an ingenious system of underfloor heating from a wood fire. There was then of course the prospect of waking up in the night facing the reality of being grilled alive.

## Crossing the Chongchon River

The Battalion was ordered to make an assault crossing of the river the day following its arrival on the Chongchon. To gain surprise it was decided to make the crossing 4 miles downstream where the river narrowed slightly. At this point the river was 800 yards wide with an approach over open paddy fields of a further 1,000 yards. An American unit would carry the assault boats down to the river and conceal them during the night. The crossing would start shortly before high tide at 0800 hours the next morning. There was nothing in intelligence reports or local information to suggest that tide or current would cause any difficulties. This intelligence was entirely faulty. Mercifully the only opposition from the North Koreans was the great press of villagers and local dignitaries who streamed down the far bank to welcome the regatta. The complete absence of the enemy allowed this assault crossing to become funny – up to a point.

The next morning we discovered that only half the assault boats had been carried down to the river and these were without paddles. Not to be deterred, the first boats pushed off at 0900 hours. They were immediately swept upstream, but eventually reached the far bank at the same time as the local mayor and great hosts of little men in white carrying enormous flags who had also experienced some difficulty in forecasting the exact point of disembarkation.

The second Company were more fortunate; a slackening tide gave them a fair run, with a less breathless concentration of local dignitaries to help them ashore. The third Company started off well, but in a few minutes the necklace of boats began to show ominous signs of sagging downstream and once more the reception committee was on the move. This Company landed on what turned out to be an island close to the far bank. By this time the tide was streaming out and soldiers had to be dragged ashore through black mud.

The fourth and last Company went one better, for this time islands of black mud were appearing. The leading boat, with Company Headquarters aboard, after grounding on pretty well every mud bank within reach, eventually made landfall 800 yards downstream, with 20 yards of mud between it and the bank. The first two over the side went straight up to their waists in the mud and it took four men to drag each one out. The remainder of the Company waited while outboard motors were fitted. These got the boats clear of the bank and then broke down. There was an interesting period when this Company was then placed with its Headquarters in the mud on the far bank, half the Company aground in midstream and the other half disappearing in the direction of the Yellow Sea.

Ultimately all were safe and sound, and by nightfall defensive positions had been occupied. There were many signs of recent enemy occupation, for the bridge had been covered by dug-in positions. Although the Battalion had safely gained its objectives, it was without its supporting arms, transport, rations and blankets.

The speed of advance and the sustained exhortation to 'barrel on' were such that there was no time for a Brigade, let alone a Divisional, plan. The 24th US Division, driving up behind, was still two days behind. After considerable collective and individual initiative sufficient boats were eventually mustered from various points in the river to enable enough supplies to be ferried across to the north bank of the river. Full use was also made of local volunteer North Koreans. The tireless efforts of our Catholic padre, Father Quinlan, in retrieving boats until well after midnight is worthy of mention.

It is strange how the fortunes of war are often so varied. When crossing the Chongchon, we were greeted by North Koreans offering us cups of tea. In contrast, the Australians who crossed the river to the west of us encountered opposition and suffered a number of casualties. The Argylls, who crossed under cover of artillery barrage, were, however, able to make considerable progress and had only minor casualties. American engineers soon successfully constructed a bridge and our vehicles and baggage were once again reunited with the Battalion, much to everyone's relief.

Two days later we were held up by some self-propelled guns and more tanks, in an action in which our tanks claimed that they had knocked out an estimated ten Korean tanks, but claims of enemy casualties usually tended to be exaggerated. I was standing on the roadside engrossed in watching the tank battle when Colonel Andrew Man ordered me to take over command of our 'C' Company immediately (a reinforcement company entirely composed of men from The Queen's Regiment and The East Surrey Regiment). Their company commander had most unfortunately been run over by one of our tanks. He had been talking on the tank external telephone situated at the rear when the tank had reversed, badly injuring one of his legs. I followed up 'C' Company on foot as fast as I could in considerable ignorance of what they were trying to achieve and feeling totally unprepared. I eventually caught up with him only to find that the Korean opposition had withdrawn.

I remained with 'C' Company until I left Korea. They were all volunteers, men with a great sense of humour and high morale. They served The Diehards with distinction, and now, 45 years after the war, still attend our Korean reunions.

*Chapter 8*

## ENTER THE CHINESE

At the end of October it was clear that the North Korean Army had been destroyed. The Commonwealth Brigade was tired and needed a rest. They were dirty, their uniforms were in rags and their few vehicles were in need of replacement. It now seemed that they would have a chance to recuperate, but there were rumours of well-clothed Chinese soldiers having been found in the nearby hills, killed by US air strikes. There were also wild rumours of vast numbers of Chinese troops said to be moving south. General MacArthur was right when he said that a new war was beginning.

On the last day of October the Chinese launched their attack. Within three or four weeks troops of the 12th, 13th and 16th Army Groups had been identified in action. The Chinese entered the war with the intention of preventing North Korea falling to the Americans and so securing China's own boundaries. Later it was estimated that some twenty-six Divisions, numbering approximately 200,000 men, had entered Korea.

The Commonwealth Brigade, in lonely insecurity on the now-deserted axis of our original advance, received reports that large forces of Chinese were converging on Taechon. This was confirmed by air reconnaissance, which showed that Chinese troops were only 4 miles away from Taechon. A number of dead Chinese had been found on the hills about Taechon, killed by air strikes. They were much larger than the Koreans and were all wearing first-class winter clothing, which included fur hats. Our own advance had previously taken us just north of Taechon and close to the Manchurian border.

The local inhabitants now reported that a force of about 200 had been in our area but had withdrawn northwards. One afternoon a Chinese was brought in who spoke English; he explained that he lived in Canton and had been lent as an instructor to the North

130

Korean Army. He now wished to give himself up as he was fed up and had no wish to fight.

On 2 November vaguely disquieting news trickled through that all was not well with the 1st Cavalry Division, who were north of Pakchon. They had been heavily attacked and suffered severe casualties, leaving some units barely able to fight at all. In the event these reports proved to be understating the reality. As more and more bad news came in there was an increasing feeling of panic among certain American units, but not, I am glad to say, in the units of the Commonwealth Brigade.

In subsequent days, when we had trucks to transport us, we usually had to put a guard on the American drivers to prevent them from driving southwards, so leaving us in the lurch. One frequently heard comments such as 'Let's get the hell out of this and drive to Pusan'. I had moments of extreme anxiety in this awesome country of high, foreboding hills. By this time the refugees had all disappeared and the only living creatures often appeared to be ourselves and the Chinese. To add to our discomfiture it was bitterly cold, with temperatures falling some 30 degrees below freezing at night. We slept fully clothed in small bivouac tents pitched in the snow.

Our feelings of uneasiness increased because it was hard to get hold of factual information. The one solid fact we were sure of was that the American 8th Army was 'bugging out' and escaping southwards. It soon became clear that the bulk of our Brigade was on its own and the only road left open for withdrawal was a lateral route that ran across our front.

Around this time my company was waiting for transport and we were occupying temporary positions astride the road, my company headquarters being in a culvert under a bridge. I was alerted to the fact that a seemingly endless column of Chinese was passing us by about half a mile away. I ordered everyone to keep still and not on any account give our position away. The Chinese were all heavily camouflaged, with what looked like natural vegetation. It put me in mind of Birnam Wood in Shakespeare's *Macbeth*.*

I believe that there are no previous instances in which British or

* 'Macbeth shall never vanquish'd be until Great Birnam wood to high Dunsinane hill shall come against him.' *Macbeth*, Act 4 Scene 1.

American troops have fought against the Chinese. We were faced with the imminent prospect of being joined in battle with soldiers of the People's Liberation Army, without information of any sort regarding their strengths and weaknesses, nor of the organization of their Army. We knew them to be tough physically, for the rank and file had an agrarian background and many years' experience fighting against the Kuomintang, the anti-Communist Chinese Nationalist Party led by General Chiang Kai-shek.

The Chinese subsequently proved to be both tough and resolute, frequently preferring to attack by night rather than by day in order to avoid the attention of the US Air Force. Their attacks were usually accompanied by a great deal of noise, including the blowing of bugles. The individual soldier carried a personal weapon and ammunition plus one week's ration (rice, tea and tinned fish or meat). Their mobility was their feet, and each soldier carried a quantity of foot-rags, which he used when his boots were worn out. Supplies were transported at night by trucks whenever possible, but more usually by enforced labour employed as porters. The daily amount of supplies (including ammunition etc.) needed by one Chinese soldier was 10 lb, compared with 60 lb for one American soldier. This crude logistical comparison between the Chinese and US ground forces says a lot.

We were now ordered to withdraw to Pakchon and, as we were without any troop-carrying transport, most of us marched. Many of the vehicles were crippled and so the column moved very slowly, nose to tail. The road was tortuous and went through a precipitous pass, where two of our ration trucks rolled off the collapsing road and finally came to rest in some trees 40 feet below. The occupants had a narrow escape, but we lost some valuable rations and carefully hoarded supplies. On entering Pakchon we, along with the rest of the Brigade, found ourselves defending the town through which the badly mauled American troops had withdrawn.

Guy Fawkes Day (5 November) dawned with the artillery to our rear defending themselves from a determined Chinese thrust designed to cut the only supply route and link to the bridge at Anju, south of which US Forces were reforming. It was a Sunday, the day of the week on which we seemed always to be fated to make some rapid move – the more elaborate the preparations made for church service, the greater the certainty of a move. So it was hardly surprising that when the brigade padre appeared that morning the Adjutant cried out, 'Keep away from us padre, there's enough trouble already as it is!'

Later in the day we were ordered to withdraw again to the Chongchon River. That day I heard that an American general, seeing our quartermaster driving northwards towards the Battalion from our administrative base some 50 miles to the south, expressed the view that nothing short of a miracle would save the 27th Commonwealth Brigade from annihilation.

On 6 November, for some extraordinary reason, the Chinese broke contact across the whole front. One theory is that they needed a respite to bring forward supplies from across the Manchurian border; another is that they were waiting to see how the Americans were going to react.

We normally saw daily American air activity, but many days in November were impossible for low-level flying because of cloud and snow. We never experienced an attack by either Korean or Chinese aircraft. However, in the later stages of the war (1951–53) some 500 MiG fighters were based north of the Manchurian border. These planes surprisingly outclassed the US F80 Shooting Star, but not the Sabre, which was the outstanding fighter plane of the war.

November was a bad month for us all. There was some talk that the fighting in Korea might become the flashpoint for World War III if Russia entered the war. There were also rumours that General MacArthur wished to use atomic weapons if the Chinese advance could not be halted by conventional means. In late November President Truman affirmed that the United States would take whatever steps were necessary to meet the military situation and that included the atomic bomb.

In a lighter vein I must mention Thanksgiving Day, which is traditionally on the fourth Thursday of November. Seldom in the history of war can so much food have descended on front-line troops – turkey by the ton, prawn cocktails by the gallon, plum cake by the truckload and tins of pumpkin pie by the gross – all to disappear down the throats of the gastronomically bewildered 'C' Ration weary troops. Some took this visitation in their stride; others were less fortunate and suffered the consequences.

Also on the brighter side of things, we managed within my Company to arrange hot water baths for everyone by the simple expedient of producing hot water in discarded 40-gallon drums: the water was heated by placing the drums over blazing log fires and then baled out into jeep trailers, which were used to bathe eight men at a time. We had to be pretty nippy, for the water cooled off very quickly. The whole process took a long time, but it meant that we had our first bath in weeks.

Another November distraction was to put out in the snow corn soaked in gin or vodka. We left it out all night and, with luck, in the morning there might be three or four drunken pheasants reeling around. The pheasants resembled the magnificent Himalayan monal pheasant. I felt sorry for the birds, but it was worth it. I never found out where the liquor came from, and in any case I thought it best not to ask.

## The Battle of the Kunuri Pass

The Kunuri Pass was the scene of the greatest defeat of our forces in the Korean War. It was where the American 2nd Division (the Indianhead Division) tried to break through 6 miles of Chinese positions in what can only be described as a 'death ride', with vehicles trying to smash their way through the burning wreckage of those who had gone before, resulting in a dreadful paralysis of command and discipline. General Marshall, who is acknowledged to be one of America's finest combat historians, has vividly described the battle in his book *The River and the Gauntlet*.* In one afternoon the Division lost 3,000 men and nearly all its transport and equipment. It took the 2nd Division many months to recover. The Divisional History described the action as a magnificent stand.

In mid-November the whole Brigade moved south across our old friend the Chongchon River to Kunuri. On 26 November the Chinese began a major offensive, and Brigadier Coad, accompanied by Major John Willoughby, one of our company commanders, visited 9 Corps Headquarters and reported that there was an atmosphere close to

---

* S.L.A. Marshall, *The River and the Gauntlet: Defeat of the Eighth Army by the Chinese Communist forces, November, 1950, in the Battle of the Chongchon River, Korea* (Westport, Conn. Greenwood Press, 1970).

panic. American divisions were marked up on a large Perspex map followed by an enigmatic question mark. In the centre pointing south was a long red arrow chinagraphed 'two million'. John Willoughby was not sure whether this was satirical or not.

The Corps Commander was uncertain how best to employ a brigade without supporting arms in this rather singular military situation and was also very concerned about the security of his main supply line running south. He therefore accepted the Brigadier's advice that this, his only reserve, would be best employed where it could protect this route. Shortly afterwards Corps Headquarters moved to Chasan, 30 miles to the south. Next morning we were ordered to follow them in transport, but, as none appeared, we set off on foot in the afternoon.

A British journalist who was present reported the start of our Brigade withdrawal through the Kunuri Pass as follows:

> The rifle companies began to form up, innocent of the fact that the new positions were 23 miles away, through the hills and directly south. The lorries and jeeps of Brigade Headquarters lurched across the frozen ground while the knife-cold wind blew away the last bits of stray paper and refuse. And then it happened: in that mean, dirty, ice-bound valley, 13,000 miles from home, came the skirl of the pipes. The Argylls, who had no more and no less sleep than anybody else, were swinging off, single file on each side of the road, but otherwise as if they were on parade.
>
> They were followed by the Australians, unfortunately newly issued with American boots. Before midnight one-third of them were destined to have no skin on their feet at all, but they were tackling this march with their usual rude cynicism. Last of all came the Middlesex, one of whom, sporting a walking-stick of all things, shouted across to me 'Say, mister, is this the right road for Piccadilly Circus?' The few vehicles and last remaining tracked carriers crawled alongside. Nothing about the weather, the scenery, the immediate future – nothing about anything presented an attractive feature. They were on the retreat and they knew it. Yet at the risk of being 'corny' there was something about the spirit of these troops as they followed the pipes, whose music curled contemptuously

through these hard, unfriendly hills, that seemed to raise them far above the ordinary run of men.

I remember clearly the eeriness of our night march. Small flakes of snow were blowing about and far away we could hear the distinctive sound of artillery fire. We marched in silence and reached the pass at midnight in bitter cold without incident. After 18 miles we were met by transport that ultimately dumped us on a windswept, frozen stretch of paddy next to Corps Headquarters. The last company arrived at 3 a.m., and in heaps of rice straw, blankets and each other, we slept. We woke up next morning with traffic pouring past us southwards. Barely had fires been lit to thaw out our tins of food than it was reported that a small roadblock was believed to have been set up near the pass by the Chinese.

The Battalion was ordered to move back to the pass again to search the area, the villages in particular, and bring in any suspicious characters. A patrol was also to go on to Kunuri and contact the US 2nd Division, which was now there. The Battalion was then to return, leaving one company in the pass. We moved back towards the pass through deserted villages along the empty road up the valley. A radio message was received that the enemy were now known to be ahead and the warning was passed up and down the column. The mountains astride the pass came into view over the top of a ridge of intermediate hills and suddenly the leading company stopped and deployed. On the side of the road, tilting into the ditch, was a bullet-ridden jeep: inside sprawled the bodies of an American colonel and his driver. I remembered passing the jeep with its grim contents during our night march. Nothing stirred and all at once the mountains about us seemed much higher, more inaccessible and more menacing. The valley ahead and the pass beyond were absolutely silent. Nothing moved except for the shift of elbows supporting binoculars, scanning every ridge and crevice above us.

Then from nowhere about twenty men in dirty white clothes appeared, strolling rather furtively towards us. Surely another second could not go by without something happening? A section ran forward and brought in three of the men. They were unarmed and gradually the tension eased. The remainder were rounded up and the leading company took up the advance. Some of us felt a little foolish. I have no idea who they were or what they were doing, but I am

136

inclined to believe that they were disguised Chinese on some form of reconnaissance.

We reached the hills and directly ahead the road climbed through the pass, disappearing after a few hundred yards and then reappearing as a long scar across the mountains. Not a soul was in sight and it seemed as if fatigue had played tricks with our instincts. We had failed to appreciate that the jeep could have given us a warning that Chinese were in the area.

However, we soon found out that the pass was not as deserted as it appeared. Five American fighters swung low over the mountains and machine-gunned the wooded slopes ahead. Chinese began to move about and gradually the fighting started: first a few rifle shots and then the steady knock of a Bren gun in reply. Our leading company pressed up the hill towards its objective. There was a short lull in the firing, then the crump of enemy mortar fire and the harsh stabbing noise of a Russian machine gun. Our Vickers machine guns took up their steady rhythmic beat and then our mortars joined in.

In the distance a small cloud of dust appeared as a lone jeep careered down the pass, jinking and bouncing from one side of the road to the other. The slopes above it came to life with the flashes of rifle fire, but still the jeep came on. It disappeared behind the shoulder of a hill; there was a further burst of fire and then silence. Then, without warning, rifle shots came from hills on the flanks and every ridge and peak about us seemed to be occupied. Mortaring became general and machine guns joined in with the rifle fire from above.

At this time the nearest troops who could possibly support the Battalion were the remainder of the Brigade, 20 miles behind us. This comprised the sum total of the Corps reserve and could not be released. In any case, radio communication with Brigade having broken down, casualties were now beginning to build up and, with darkness approaching, there was an increasing danger of being cut off. The decision was made to withdraw.

As the Battalion was coming back communication with Brigade was re-established and we received a message that we were to withdraw well clear of the pass to a defensive position 8 miles to the south. The Battalion was extricated with some difficulty, with its transport under fire from the rear. My company finally left after a hand-to-hand fight with the Chinese. One of my sergeants was credited with killing a Chinese soldier with a spade. It was dark by the time we reached our position for the night and the best that could be done was to occupy a tight perimeter round the village and hope that daylight would not reveal too many overlooking hills. We then received information that a US Regimental combat team would pass through us the next morning to link up with the 2nd Infantry Division, but this news was no sooner received than it was cancelled. Once again we were on our own, with the prospect of having to return to the pass the next day.

Soon after daybreak we received orders to return to the pass, my company on the right and John Willoughby's company on the left, each with a platoon of tanks and some gunner support (newly arrived). It was strange to be returning for the second time. It was highly likely that there would be greatly increased air activity in support of the American 2nd Division and I made doubly sure that we had our fluorescent air identification panels with us. The possibility of being a target for a napalm air attack was too horrific to contemplate.

All was quiet and we waited to see whether the 2nd Division's breakout would be an infantry sweep east or west to open the road. A small column of tanks with one or two jeeps appeared and streaked down towards us, disappearing and then reappearing round the bend in a fusillade of shots, and reached our lines. Then, to our astonishment, a long nose-to-tail column appeared at the top of the pass. We concluded that the Chinese must have gone, but the gathering noise of firing made it clear that this was not so. The endless column of American vehicles came on until the bend hid them and then stopped. Through binoculars we could see the occupants jumping out and diving for cover. A few jeeps reappeared below us and careered past, firing at us thinking that we were Chinese. They went by with wounded and dead hanging out of the side of their vehicles and their tyres shot to ribbons.

Meanwhile our tanks and artillery were giving what support was possible. Aircraft were machine-gunning and bombing the Chinese. A trickle of vehicles attempted to pass the halted column and a few of these reached us, but in a very short time the column was double-banked and nothing moved.

A stream of survivors now started to come through from the valley below. Many were wounded; all were bewildered and shocked. Occasional vehicles continued to come through, all with their burden of dead and wounded. By late afternoon the pass was still again and the stream of survivors had almost stopped. We were now ordered to withdraw. As we made our way to our transport on the road below us firing once again broke out from the hills about us. As the first company was preparing to drive off we came under machine-gun fire from a ridge immediately to our left. The guns replied over open sights to be joined later by the Vickers guns and some tanks. By this time bullets were coming from all directions and the road was under fire. We withdrew with difficulty; the guns were extricated without loss and we started our return to Chasan, our vehicles packed with American wounded. As we drove through the village where we had spent the night we passed a temporary aid post. This was manned by our medical sergeant, who had treated over 250 wounded and had used all the Battalion's supplies of morphia and dressings, while others distributed among the wounded their own blankets and tea and sugar rations. Many could not be treated and during the night much of our transport was used to ferry them back to other medical units. We had to leave a great many dead behind. Back at Chasan our medical officer worked all night on other wounded Americans, who were brought straight there.

Meanwhile 9 Corps Headquarters had moved south of Pyongyang. Trucks, tanks and transporters streamed by all night and all through the next day in an endless jumble and confusion of units. Everyone was driving for all they were worth to south of Pyongyang – to where? Nobody knew. It was impossible to tell what was happening and everything had the appearance of a rout.

## The Great Bug-Out

The United States Army was now fleeing southwards, abandoning much of its equipment, and individual soldiers discarded some of their personal equipment in order to lighten their load. General Walker's 8th Army withdrew approximately 120 miles in 10 days, recrossing the 38th Parallel on 15 December, pursued by Chinese soldiers. Generally speaking they were ill-armed and moving on their feet, without air support. In Pyongyang, the Army's main forward base, vast supply dumps were burnt and pillars of smoke could be seen for miles around.

In early December Brigadier Coad sent a signal to the British Commander-in-Chief, Far East, painting a grim picture of the state of his Brigade and the difficulties of operating effectively with the Americans. The reply came, 'Stick it out', which we all did.

At this stage the principal victims of the war were the civilians, who were struggling south along all available roads and tracks. To add to their misery they were frequently strafed by American fighter planes. The dusty narrow roads of North Korea were packed tight with vehicles of all descriptions moving southwards.

The wind had dropped and it had stopped snowing, but the sky was heavy. The white sameness of the landscape was broken only by the black crags and cliff faces of the mountains. Throughout our withdrawal we received frequent reports of Chinese following us up. On one occasion we were informed that a large force of Chinese were in our area but not a single Chinese had been seen anywhere by us. An Australian patrol had found one dead cow and two dead civilians where the Air Force claimed to have wiped out an enemy battalion, but that was all. For some time we had felt that the intelligence evaluations were getting a bit out of hand and were conducive to spreading alarm.

We skirted the eastern suburbs of Pyongyang. The place looked, if possible, more gaunt and miserable than it had seemed to us less than two months previously on our way north. The great girder bridges over the river still lay broken and twisted and beyond them black columns of smoke showed where military stores were being burnt. It was a discouraging scene of desolation and abandonment. The road south-east led across an open plain and into the mountain mass of central Korea, at that time marked on situation maps with a red circle enclosing the sinister phrase 'Concentration of organized guerrillas'. If there were guerrillas they could only have been North Korean, but my guess is that they never existed.

The wind returned and blew remorselessly. For those hanging on to mudguards and jeep trailers it was a test of endurance. As our column moved slowly on we began to overtake the retreating ROK Army (Republic of Korea). They were a wretched and dispiriting sight, struggling back in ragged and varied uniforms. They had no transport of any sort and must have been trudging southward for many days.

Somewhere south of Pyongyang we met up with the recently arrived and well-equipped 29th Brigade from the UK – our 'brothers in arms'. In the early days, rightly or wrongly, we had assumed that the arrival of this brigade would be the signal for our return to Hong Kong. It had therefore been rather natural, in our tired and more forlorn moments, to natter 'Come on, 29th Brigade'. In fact, once or twice a few had even gone so far as to suggest that they were a bit slow in arriving. However, by all reports, they were a strong, independent brigade group with the latest arms and equipment, a real showpiece. Thus they had come to be known by us as the 'Festival of Britain boys'.

Here they were at last, caught up in the same stupendous military mess-up as ourselves. We were delighted to see them and they gave us a fine welcome as we passed through. Pretty well every basic sentiment and rugged epithet was joyfully hurled from one side to the other. The colourful texture of the soldier's vocabulary could not have been better displayed. Englishmen are not as a rule so communicative to each other when they meet in foreign countries; Dr Livingstone would have been badly shaken. The 29th Brigade looked smart and business-like. We must have appeared a strange contrast to them, in our worn and dusty assortment of American and British winter clothing.

The dust was awful. The cold was worse. At every enforced halt we searched around for dead wood or grass and lit a fire. Sometimes we were lucky in stopping by a blazing fire already lit by those ahead of us who had moved on. The crowd pressing in invariably resulted in scorched clothes. But it was worth it; almost anything would have been worth it. At one halt a truck carrying ROKs drew into the side and the occupants offered a lift to a refugee and his wife with one small child. Their bedding, all they possessed, was flung on to the lorry. Just at that moment the traffic moved on without them, taking the bedding with it. It was 1 a.m.

On 10 December we recrossed the 38th Parallel. It was very early morning and scarcely light when my jeep driver woke me up. I looked with interest to see whether the sign that we had erected some two months previously was still there to be seen: 'The Mids can say with glee and joy that they were here before Kilroy'. There was no trace of it, but much to my amusement I saw a new sign, which said:

You are recrossing the 38th Parallel by courtesy of the Chinese People's Liberation Army.

Ever since Kunuri, which seemed like a thousand years ago, we had been deprived of humour. The fact that some American soldier had put this sign up cheered us all immensely. If I had had a camera and immediate access to the Press I could have made a fortune with the newspapers of the world.

We finally came to roost in the foothills just north of a completely ruined town with the delightful name of Uijongbu, only some 15 miles north of Seoul. It was in this area that we stayed until New Year's Day. As Christmas drew near, and the wags were talking of the dwindling number of shopping days left, we learned that, Chinese permitting, we would be spending Christmas just where we were. We were bivouacked in a series of adjacent small valleys. It had snowed frequently and, while this made the countryside quite attractive scenically, the hard ground and low temperatures made living in the open devoid of appeal.

By Christmas Eve we were prepared to enjoy the occasion with some degree of comfort. Without direct orders or obvious organization, but with great enthusiasm and in a competitive spirit, there appeared on this bleak mountainside an array of shacks and huts of which Peacehaven or Canvey Island could be proud. These erections could not have passed the critical eye of a borough architect, but they were warm and dry and often tastefully decorated within with Christmas cards and pin-ups. Something more than covering and warmth was needed to complete our Christmas and we were not disappointed. Parcels and letters arrived from well-wishers throughout England. We were cheered immensely by this very practical sign of affectionate interest shown by our hitherto unknown friends.

The arrangements for mail, both inward and outward, worked remarkably well, considering the circumstances. Corry and I were able to keep in touch using Air Mail Active Service Letter Forms for brief correspondence. I have a letter dated 20 December 1950 in which I wrote:

I am living in an improvised shelter made from coconut matting, planks of wood and corrugated iron. A squatter's hut

'Gookery Nook'

in Hong Kong is indeed a palace in comparison to mine but I am houseproud nonetheless. I have named it 'Gookery Nook'.*

There was nothing in the various intelligence reports to cause us any alarm, so we set about doing what the Army calls 'make and mend': maintaining vehicles, arms and equipment, and relaxing whenever possible. The main aim was to give our soldiers as good a Christmas as possible. The officers and sergeants hosted separate drinks parties for representatives throughout the Brigade. A large marquee appeared from somewhere and a gigantic bonfire was kept going just outside. The Americans provided the most lavish Christmas fare for all ranks in their rations, complete with turkey and Christmas pudding. The Diehards had mastered the circumstances and enjoyed a 'Merrie' traditional Christmas.

When Brigadier Coad was visiting the warrant officers and sergeants at Christmas he was approached by the impressive figure of the Regimental Sergeant Major of the Australians, who said, 'Our "Diggers" think a hell of a lot of you, Sir'. The Brigadier was obviously somewhat embarrassed by this. The RSM continued: 'Sir, there is not a single man, who, when he sees you, does not say "Here comes that ―――― white-haired old bastard."' By this time the Brigadier was more than taken aback. The RSM hastily reassured him that such language was a term of great respect and endearment in his Army.

It may seem strange, but some of us who realized what a humiliating defeat we had all suffered felt slightly uneasy at the surfeit of food and the feasting. Perhaps the Americans offered it as a form of propitiation, but I doubt it.

Just before Christmas an event took place that was ultimately to affect the course of the war. General Walker, the 8th Army Commander, was on his way from his own Headquarters to visit our Brigade when his vehicle collided with an ROK truck and he was killed. He was at this time a weary and disillusioned man as a result of the collapse of his Army. He was almost immediately replaced by

* The term 'gook' is a slang word for anyone of Asiatic origin. It was widely used throughout the Korean War, particularly by the Americans.

General Ridgway, a born leader and paratrooper. One of the purposes of General Walker's visit was to present to us a medal in recognition of our defence of the Pusan bridgehead after our arrival in South Korea. We never received the medal, which was a pity, for it was highly original: the actual ribbon depicted what looked like two copulating whales but in fact represented the national emblem of South Korea.

## Where Men are Men

The human race is three at least,
The Man, the Woman and the Beast,
And in the palimpsest of years
It is the man who always wears
The trousers in his married home
Be it of mud or castled stone.

But now it is the woman's claim
That Man and Beast are just the same.
Only there stays within his thrall
The hatstand in the entrance hall.
One solitary island there
Of purely masculine wear.

A pity thus that Man should bear
These silly symbols of despair,
Disreputably old and stained
Three times discarded, thrice regained-
His self respect has joined the dead
Felt albatross about his head.

But travel eastwards to Korea
Where Men are Men and Women wear
A different kind of trousers here.
And you can see them by the scores
Cutting the wood and scrubbing floors,
While sitting in the sun on mats
Are all the men in marvellous hats

In Uijongbu they affect
A style portraying intellect
While on the Naktong there are rows
Of chimneyed hats black as the crows
And strangely perforated too
To let their wisdom vapour through.

John Willoughby
Christmas 1950

*Note*: This poem was composed principally to the memory of Korean hats, many of which were a status symbol of some sort, in particular the chimney hats of the village elders. Alas, today with the passing of time and the Americanization of South Korea, they are to be seen no more. Perhaps Men are no longer Men!

## The Chinese Capture Seoul

After Christmas the number of Chinese troops north of the Parallel was reported to be increasing. Seoul was in a state of panic and everyone was getting out as fast as they could.

During the first few hours of the New Year the Chinese forced an ROK division to the north of us to retreat in disorder. At first light we were ordered to move north to take up positions through which the ROK division could retreat and thereafter to act as rearguard until another position could be established south of Uijongbu. The progress of the Chinese advance could be roughly followed from the behaviour of American fighter aircraft circling ahead and sweeping in to machine-gun and rocket the Chinese.

The last of the air-strikes took place in the twilight, pouring cannon fire, rockets and napalm bombs into the broken ground and villages immediately to our front. To our left the barren mountains made a ragged outline against the western sky. On our right the last of the refugees had disappeared southwards down the railway line and, beyond, another range of mountains straggled up into the night. Ahead glowed the flames from burning villages. A number of out-wardly mundane subjects were exercising the minds of our soldiers. First, because it immediately concerned them, was the performance of the new individual cookers. The hesitant blue flames flickering at the bottom of the trench were the subject of much earnest conjectures and profound philosophy. Second, because it should have immediately concerned them, was the fate of some twenty fat turkeys that had been carefully kept refrigerated in the snow for New Year's dinner and were now goodness knows where. Third, as a sort of obligato to the other two, were the football results just received on typed sheets from our rear Headquarters.

At midnight we started to move back, company by company. There was some delay in getting the vehicles out of the frozen paddy and up the icy banks on to the road. An ambulance rolled over onto its side and blocked the exit for a time, but there was no interference from the Chinese and the whole Battalion got safely through to the suburbs of Seoul. By daybreak the Brigade was concentrated amongst the bombed-out schools and other buildings in the northern outskirts of Seoul.

The following day the Chinese broke through and the situation rapidly began to become very fluid, with some air strikes being made in error on us. In the afternoon we were ordered to take up a rearguard position to cover the main forces through Seoul and across the Han River. This was a task for which we had been warned before Christmas and we had already made a detailed reconnaissance of positions covering the main easterly bridge over the Han River. However, it is in the nature of withdrawals that new plans are produced at the last moment and we were eventually required to use the westerly bridge. The new plan required us to hold the high ground and about three-quarters of the ridge overlooking Seoul, while the Australians held the remainder and blocked the main road. The Argylls were to hold the Chinese to the north of the city. Eventually, when the main body of 9 Corps were through, they were to withdraw into the city and provide close protection for the bridge. We and the Australians would then withdraw through them.

These positions were hastily reconnoitred and in the failing light we struggled and clambered up into the mountains and were soon swallowed up in the night. From these rocky spurs looking down on Seoul we could see a great pall of smoke hanging over the city. Several large fires were burning and many tall buildings were silhouetted against the flames. The sweat from our climbing was frozen on us. The warmth from our boots had thawed the snow and our feet were soaking. Now our boots were freezing on our wet feet. We were also very hungry. Moscow must have felt and looked like this to Napoleon's army. Far down below us in the warmth and shelter of Battalion Headquarters a bugler sounded the cookhouse call: 'Come to the cookhouse door, boys'. The call floated up to us, evoking a vision of the inequalities of life. This incident drifted innocently into a beautiful Fleet Street legend of the British rearguards defying the Chinese buglers with their own. Perhaps we imagined the whole incident.

For those of us without any bedding in the mountains above Seoul this was the coldest and worst night in Korea. There was a great sense of drama; we knew that the Chinese were closing in and were about to capture the capital city of South Korea, but we could not withdraw until ordered to do so. To add to our problems there was very little vegetation to give us any cover and the ground was so solidly frozen that it was impossible to dig in. The only option was to hope and pray. Some time before midnight the Australian outposts were withdrawn.

It was estimated that the bulk of the main forces would be clear of Seoul before daylight. This would allow us to withdraw shortly afterwards. Exchanges of mortar and machine-gun fire between the Australians and the Chinese continued during the night, but the Battalion was warned to prepare to hold its present position for a further twelve hours. Three hours later the orders were changed once again and the Australians were told that we would follow them when they were clear. It was well after 9 o'clock before all our companies were down off the hills and had formed up in a mixed column of tanks, trucks and carriers in the city's outskirts. The column eventually moved off through the deserted city and crossed the Han River.

At the time we were relieved to pass across the Han River, for it was a significant stepping stone on our withdrawal south, but I also felt a sense of shame that our previous successes had been in vain and that we had had to leave some of our dead behind us in North Korea.

Near the bridge I met someone from our Rear Headquarters who gave me a parcel from Corry, posted in Hong Kong, containing tins of caviar and *paté de fois gras*. God bless her. I had written some weeks previously to say that I had a craving for some luxuries. Also on the bridge I found to my amazement a troop of Centurion tanks from a squadron of The King's Royal Irish Hussars, looking smart and efficient. They had come to Korea with the newly formed 29 Infantry Brigade. I climbed aboard the troop leader's tank to have a brief chat and shared a tin of caviar with him, which we ate with dry biscuits.

I recently (1998) asked Colonel Andrew Man, the only surviving senior officer in the Brigade, how it was that we came to carry out the vital role of rearguard covering the evacuation of Seoul. He told me that the Americans had a very high regard for Brigadier Coad and his Brigade, and asked him to undertake the task.

All of us in the rearguard breathed a well-earned sigh of relief when we were safely across the Han River, for there were so many things that could have gone wrong. I remember becoming a prisoner of my own fears in imagining that the bridges might possibly be prematurely destroyed by some over-eager and 'windy' demolition commander. However, I was prudent and kept my thoughts to myself. I would like to know at what time the Chinese leading troops entered Seoul. The answer is purely academic, but interesting none-theless; my guess is that they were hard on our heels.

## South of Seoul

In some indefinable way many of us thought that life south of the Han River might be different. Perhaps logistic weaknesses might have forced the Chinese to run out of steam and sought a ceasefire. Perhaps General MacArthur, being a strong advocate for dropping an atomic bomb on China *pour décourager la guerre*, might actually do so. This would have had the effect of either dramatically ending the war or escalating it into World War III. This latter thought was in fact not far off the mark, for in early April General MacArthur was to openly criticize President Truman for adopting a strategy of war limitation. On 11 April President Truman relieved General MacArthur of his UN command.

Whatever our thoughts, most of us were of the opinion that the war would now end sooner rather than later. If on New Year's Day we had been faced with the hypothesis that the war might continue for another year and a half, resulting in the deaths of thousands more combatants on both sides and would finally end approximately on the line where it first began, the 38th Parallel, we would have found it totally beyond belief.

Once over the river we found ourselves at the tail-end of a long column of halted vehicles and we were given the customary 'bug-out' instructions as to our escape route. To use the term 'escape route' was, to say the least, a psychological madness. After various moves and reconnaissances of defence lines further back, and after having travelled 120 miles by road, we finally wound up only 40 miles from Seoul.

Because we were operating on a minimum of transport, we were limited to one blanket a man, which was totally inadequate as the temperature was continuously well below freezing; once it touched minus 40° Fahrenheit. Fortunately we were in an area where there were a number of abandoned villages and we occupied wooden houses that had a marvellous underfloor heating system using burning logs; we had of course used the system before.

In early February Colonel Andrew Man told me that I would very shortly be returning to England to become an instructor at the School of Infantry at Warminster. I would, of course, be going back via Hong Kong and Corry, and we would then return home together by ship soon after the birth of our second child. The reason for the posting was that they wanted an instructor with experience as a company commander fighting the Chinese. I thought it slightly ironic that I had only a few years previously spent a large part of World War II fighting the Japanese.

Just before I left the Battalion there was increased Chinese activity on our front and all our Companies were involved. Below are extracts from a letter sent to the Colonel of the Regiment by John Willoughby:

'Stand-to' was ordered at 0400, by which time the moon had set. At 0510 the Chinese came in, supported by mortars and machine guns, blowing bugles and small tin trumpets, sounding like the call of a pheasant, and calling out 'Are you English?' From then on until 0645 there was no respite.

It is quite impossible to describe accurately or in detail what happened in that time. The main attacks, which came in waves, fell on 'A' and 'D' Companies. One platoon of 'A' Company was overrun after they had run out of ammunition – one section was temporarily taken prisoner while the remaining two sections managed to pull back onto higher ground and carry on the fight. Everyone stood their ground and there were many cases of hand-to-hand fighting. Stanley Fothergill's batman had his rifle taken from him by two Chinese, but in the mêlée managed to seize one of their tommy-guns and killed them both. The mortar FOO's* radio had a grenade through it very early on and the only means of communication we had with the Company was via the New Zealand FOO, Lieutenant Roxburgh, who put up a wonderful show throughout – shooting with one hand and working his radio with the other.

It is no good my picking out individuals for praise – they were all wonderful, and the sight next morning with 48 dead Chinese right in the Company area is past all description. As I went round at first light, I was met everywhere with broad grins, our wounded coming back to the RAP,* all laughing and joking, men firing at the retreating Chinese in the valley, soldiers standing up and cheering as our prisoners came back, having broken away from their captors. I believe it was the most exhilarating moment of my life. We learnt later from interrogated prisoners – we took twelve – that it was a battalion attack. They certainly meant to stay, as they had brought picks and shovels and their medical unit.

Roxburgh was subsequently awarded the Military Cross for this action.


## Final Weeks

The question of when our relief and return to Hong Kong would take place was one that had touched and sorely tried the Battalion on two previous occasions, when it was bitterly disappointed on the eve of its scheduled departure. Fate was yet to play this scurvy trick a third time. There was no more controversial subject in the Brigade.

* Forward observation officer.
* Regimental aid post.

It is understandable therefore that rumour, the spice of the soldiers' life, was ever rife and that the most innocent of factors were distorted, grew apace, became typhonic and then blew themselves out only to be replaced by some equally fantastic rumour.

I left the Battalion in mid-February in much the same way as I had arrived, except that I was not carrying my golf clubs and tennis racquet. I had mixed feelings about getting an easy ticket back to Hong Kong. The following anecdote concerning the commanding officer of a well-known cavalry regiment, which arrived in Korea much later than ourselves, caused me much amusement. While his unit prepared their Centurion tanks for embarkation, he issued his own hints to officers about their personal preparations. He suggested taking fishing gear, four rolls of lavatory paper and a shotgun – 'though not your best shotgun' – and ammunition, 'because Eley cartridges may be difficult to obtain'.

During March the Chinese began to withdraw northwards towards the Han River and Seoul. The 8th Army reacted by edging forward, spurred by a new confidence and enthusiasm instilled by General Ridgway. The war news continued to be good, with the Chinese withdrawing on all fronts, but nevertheless intelligence reports indicated an ever-increasing build-up some few miles north of the battle line and warned that the long-expected spring offensive was imminent. One more bizarre report contained a first-hand description of how the Chinese were training large numbers of grenade-carrying guerrillas, who were to spearhead the attack and throw horror and confusion into the ranks of the United Nations.

There followed a series of Brigade operations in conjunction with the American 24th Division. We gave better than we got, but sadly suffered a number of casualties. The terrain was difficult and the weather atrocious, with frequent snowstorms. After one particular attack by the Chinese, one company of the Australians counted 120 dead Chinese in their area and took forty prisoners.

There were many false alarms and excursions before the Battalion finally embarked on 14 May at the port of Inchon on an American landing ship bound for Hong Kong. The 27th Commonwealth Brigade had been replaced by a new British Brigade (the 28th). The Port Authority at Inchon, obviously aware that no one had been able to use a proper lavatory seat for many months, provided many seats, but alas no buckets.

It was now all over and Korea would soon be only a memory. Today, some 46 years later, there are only a few who had any experience of what it was like to campaign in the bitter Siberian cold, to the very borders of China. For The Diehards it had been a campaign of swift advances and equally rapid retreat over great distances, most of it across the frozen rivers and mountains of North Korea.

We who were there would be left with nostalgic memories: 1st Cavalry Boulevard,* the ambiguous and ubiquitous Kilroy and a host of other incidents and characters. It had also been a period of tough fighting against a resolute enemy under terrible conditions. These reminiscences are above else about courage and endurance of 'comrades in arms'.

Finally, none of our achievements would have been possible without our American friends, who generally bore the main weight of the fighting and provided our fire and logistic support, and whose Air Force allowed us to campaign free of either North Korea or Chinese air attack.

Later the 1st Commonwealth Division came into being on 28 July 1952 when defensive positions were stabilized on the general line of the '38th Parallel'.

## Casualties

Considering the time that we spent in the front line, our casualties were not as heavy as they might have been. They totalled 136 killed and wounded, all ranks. Six young officers were killed leading their platoons, and thirty-six other ranks were killed; the rest were wounded.

We had a run of good luck. For example, it was little short of a miracle that we marched through the Kunuri Pass unscathed, for it could so easily have been a bloodbath. Again, when my Company was withdrawing north of Pakchon, we were passed by a seemingly endless column of Chinese, only half a mile away, camouflaged with foliage. We could have met head-on.

---

\* A term used for any route taken by the 1st Cavalry Division.

But the most important factor that reduced casualties was the leadership of our senior officers, particularly Brigadier Basil Coad, our Brigade Commander. The discipline of our soldiers also had a direct bearing on casualties. It prevented needless medical casualties, particularly frostbite, which was the scourge of some other units.

# EPILOGUE

As there were no scheduled flights to Hong Kong I had to wait a couple of days at Iwakuni US Air Base in Japan. Eventually I got a seat in a US Navy plane and was so excited that I nearly left my baggage behind, not that it would have mattered, for it was only a load of dirty old rubbish. Then it was back to a home that I had never seen before. I can't adequately describe how marvellous it was to see Corry again. We had been apart for nearly seven months: not a long time, but it had seemed like half a lifetime, for we had been already separated for nearly a year before Corry travelled out by ship to join me. And then after only four months she had found herself on her own, living in one room in a hotel. P.J. had grown beyond recognition, and Corry, now expecting our second child, was looking marvellous and in rude health.

Our house was an attractive army quarter in a small quiet terrace not far from the harbour in Kowloon. It had a tiny front garden with a privet hedge and looked out on to some palm trees. Such places no longer exist in Kowloon today; they have been replaced by skyscrapers. When we returned on a sentimental visit some years later the whole landscape was different and there was little that we could recognize.

For those few short weeks living together in Kowloon our life was comfortable. We had a Chinese *amah* by the name of Ah Seng, who was young and willing, plus an older Chinese woman as a cook-cum-general factotum with the intriguing name of Ah Ee. It was for us both a short period of pure delight, probably more so for me coming straight out of Korea.

While Corry was on her own, she worked as a secretary for the British Labour Attaché accredited to the British Foreign Office in Peking. His 'office' was a hotel room in the Peninsula Hotel in

Kowloon. She travelled to and from her work in a rickshaw drawn by a Chinese. There are no rickshaws to be seen today.

One evening, soon after my return, I heard a considerable commotion going on in our front garden. I went outside to find a number of policemen rummaging about in the bushes. Jokingly, I said to a British police inspector: 'If you are looking for a body you will find it in the bushes'. He replied: 'How did you know that it was there?' It transpired that a Chinese Nationalist general and a leading member of the Kuomintang (Chinese Nationalist Party) had been assassinated, presumably by Chinese communist agents. Why the body was dumped in our garden, I shall never know.

Michael, our second son, made a much belated entry into the world, and so delayed our departure to the UK. It was not until early May that the medical authorities would give us clearance to move. We returned home as a family of four on the troopship *Dunera*, the same ship in which the Battalion had sailed to Hong Kong two years previously.

My story has covered a period of some twelve years, embracing two wars, both in the Far East. These years saw my transition from schoolboy to professional soldier. Strange to say, the wars in Burma and Korea, although separated in time, have in my mind a certain unexplainable continuity and inevitability. Out of the maelstrom of the fighting grew the conviction that I wanted to pursue the career of being a regular soldier. The Army's inherent spirit and comradeship, mixed with liberal doses of good humour, was a brew I could not resist.

I am grateful for the experience of having served with fine soldiers, both Indian and British. I was most fortunate to marry a wife who so loyally supported me throughout a sometimes turbulent and exciting career, covering some 35 years, often having to live in remote and strange places.

If I was to be asked the question 'Would you do it all again?', my answer would be an unhesitating 'Yes', given, of course, the same conditions and circumstances, and the opportunity to balance the good with the bad.

*Appendix*

## BRITISH SOLDIERS IN KOREA

'Britain's reluctant warriors in Korea' was the headline over a full two-page article in the *Sunday Telegraph* of 13 September 1987. Max Hastings, Editor of the *Daily Telegraph*, had just written a major book* about the Korean war. In this edited pre-publication extract he described the chaos of the British recall of reservists and the bitterness it engendered. Quite understandably, many interpreted the headline in the very general sense that those soldiers serving in Korea were reluctant to do so. The article was in fact referring to the call-up of reservists in categories who were required for specialist roles in the Navy, Army and Air Force. As far as I am aware we had only a handful of reservists in the Battalion.

Britain never confronted the Korean War in the same wholehearted way in which the Americans did. The war remained an unpopular one. With reluctance the decision was, however, made that a land force of at least one brigade should be sent. Many reservists were recalled to the colours, often without logic or compassion and it was these who formed the rump of discontent.

At the time of the Korean War approximately 60% of our soldiers in the Battalion were National Servicemen, who had been enlisted for 18 months' service; the large majority were private soldiers and lance-corporals, with a few making the rank of corporal. It was during the war that the period of National Service was increased to two years.

In September 1987 I wrote to Max Hastings on the subject of 'Reluctant Warriors'. He replied as follows:

* Max Hastings, *The Korean War* (London: Joseph, 1987).

157

Thank you for your most interesting letter. I am bound to say that among the many Korean veterans I interviewed, I found more than a few who had ambivalent attitudes to Korea both at the time and since.

I hope that you will find my book as a whole reasonably balanced. I got General Tony Farrar-Hockley to read the manuscript to make sure I had not made many awful errors. I also had the pleasure of reading your own book on *The Diehards in Korea*.

I do not think the *Sunday Telegraph* will be able to run your letter as it stands, because it is so clearly addressed to me personally. But I am equally sure that they will be interested in some version written explicitly for publication, and addressed to their Letters Editor.

Thank you so much anyway for taking the trouble to write.

In early October, the Editor of the *Sunday Telegraph* published my letter:

### The Valour of Our Korean Battalions

I have read with great interest the edited pre-publication extracts from Max Hastings' book *The Korean War*. These convey the strong impression that the majority of National Servicemen and reservists sent to Korea were 'reluctant warriors'.

Furthermore, according to one company commander in the Commonwealth Brigade (1st Battalion the Middlesex Regiment), 'soldiers seemed in a state of shock for many weeks after we arrived'.

I too was a company commander in the same battalion and served throughout the most exacting period of the war. I found no reluctant soldiers, either in my battalion or in that magnificent battalion of the Argyll and Sutherland Highlanders, who fought alongside us all the way. Our story is one of courage and endurance of 'comrades in arms' borne along by sharp Cockney wit and dour Scottish humour.

Another extracted comment: 'I was worried about the

Americans and know what a mess they could get into', implies a great deal. Most of us had the greatest respect for the Americans, who generally bore the main weight of the fighting and provided during those early days our fire and logistical support, and whose air superiority allowed us to campaign free of air attack.

I am sure that Max Hastings's book provides a more balanced picture, but selective editing of various interviews inevitably gives a distorted picture. The headline 'Privations of almost Crimean proportions' is also misleading. Of course it was tough and we were initially ill-equipped for the intense cold, but, unlike the Crimea, we had able leaders, good discipline, US combat rations and good medical support. We had little time to feel sorry for ourselves. Having said all this it is understandable that many of us had ambivalent attitudes to Korea both at the time and since.

# INDEX